# This book belongs to

*Published by*

CALLAWAY ARTS & ENTERTAINMENT
76 Georgica Road, East Hampton, New York 11937

Nicholas Callaway, *CEO & Publisher* • Manuela Roosevelt, *Associate Publisher and Editorial Director* • True Sims, *Production Director*
Toshiya Masuda, *Art Director* • Ivan Wong, *Production Manager* • Jason Brown, *Graphic Design & Production* • Janice Fisher, *Proofreading*

All rights reserved.

No part of this book may be reproduced or transmitted in any form or by any means, electronic or mechanical, including photocopying, recording, or by any information storage and retrieval system, without permission in writing from the publisher.

Callaway and the Callaway logotype, and Callaway Arts & Entertainment are trademarks.

Copyright © 2024 by Michael Hoffen, Christian Casey, Jen Thum
Design, typography, and image selection by Michael Hoffen and Christian Casey
Front cover design by Joel Tippie

Printed in Canada

Distributed by Hachette Book Group in the US and Canada and by Thames & Hudson outside of North America

First Edition
1 3 5 7 9 10 8 6 4 2

Library of Congress Control Number: 2023951332

ISBN 979-8-9874124-3-5

# BE A SCRIBE!

## Working for a Better Life in Ancient Egypt

Michael Hoffen, Christian Casey, Jen Thum

NEW YORK 2024

# CONTENTS

Introduction 6
Ancient Egyptian 8
Timeline 12
Map 14

**Journey** **16**
On the River 18
Fatherly Advice 20
The Best Job 22

**Jobs** **24**
The Smith 26
The Carpenter 28
The Jeweler 30
The Barber 32
The Trader 34
The Potter 36
The Wall Builder 38
The Roofer 40
The Gardener 42
The Tenant Farmer 44
The Weaver 46
The Weapon Maker 48

The Courier 50
The Leather Worker 52
The Sandal Maker 54
The Launderer 56
The Bird Catcher 58
The Fisherman 60

**Wisdom** **62**
Be a Scribe! 64
Stay Out of Trouble... 66
Mind Your Manners 68
Don't Blab! 70
Don't Play Hooky 72
Follow Orders 74
Control Yourself 76
Be Gumptious 78
Fate Is Your Friend 80

Acknowledgments 82
Learn More 82
About the Images 83
About the Authors 94
Index 95

# INTRODUCTION

Have you ever wondered what ordinary life was like in ancient Egypt? If so, this is the book for you! It will take you on a journey through the hopes, fears, struggles, and skills of the ancient people who lived in the shadows of the pyramids.

This is the story of a father, Khety, bringing his son, Pepi, up the Nile to a school far away so that he can learn to read and write. With those skills, Pepi might have a chance at a better life as a scribe in the royal court. In order to make sure his son studies hard and learns as much as he can, Khety tells him about the many terrible other jobs that he might get if he isn't hired as a scribe. He lists 18 of them, all of which you'll learn about here. Along the way, Khety gives Pepi some fatherly wisdom to help him navigate the dangerous environment of the capital city on his own.

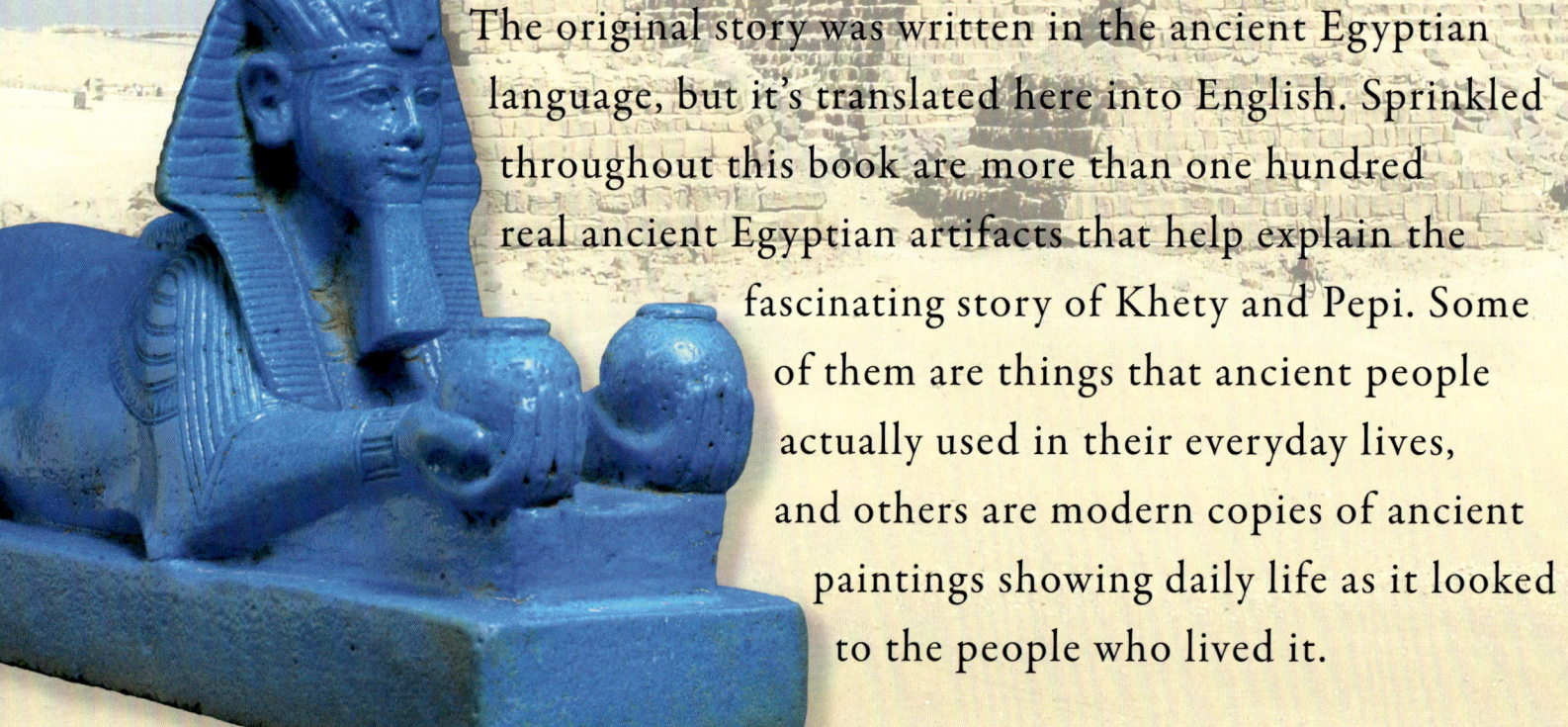

The original story was written in the ancient Egyptian language, but it's translated here into English. Sprinkled throughout this book are more than one hundred real ancient Egyptian artifacts that help explain the fascinating story of Khety and Pepi. Some of them are things that ancient people actually used in their everyday lives, and others are modern copies of ancient paintings showing daily life as it looked to the people who lived it.

This story takes place during the time we call the Middle Kingdom (see page 12), almost 4,000 years ago. Since it is thousands of years old, it can sometimes be hard to understand. Whenever things get tricky, you'll find helpful information to explain what's going on.

Spend enough time flipping through these pages, and by the end, you'll have a pretty clear understanding of what it was like to be an ancient Egyptian!

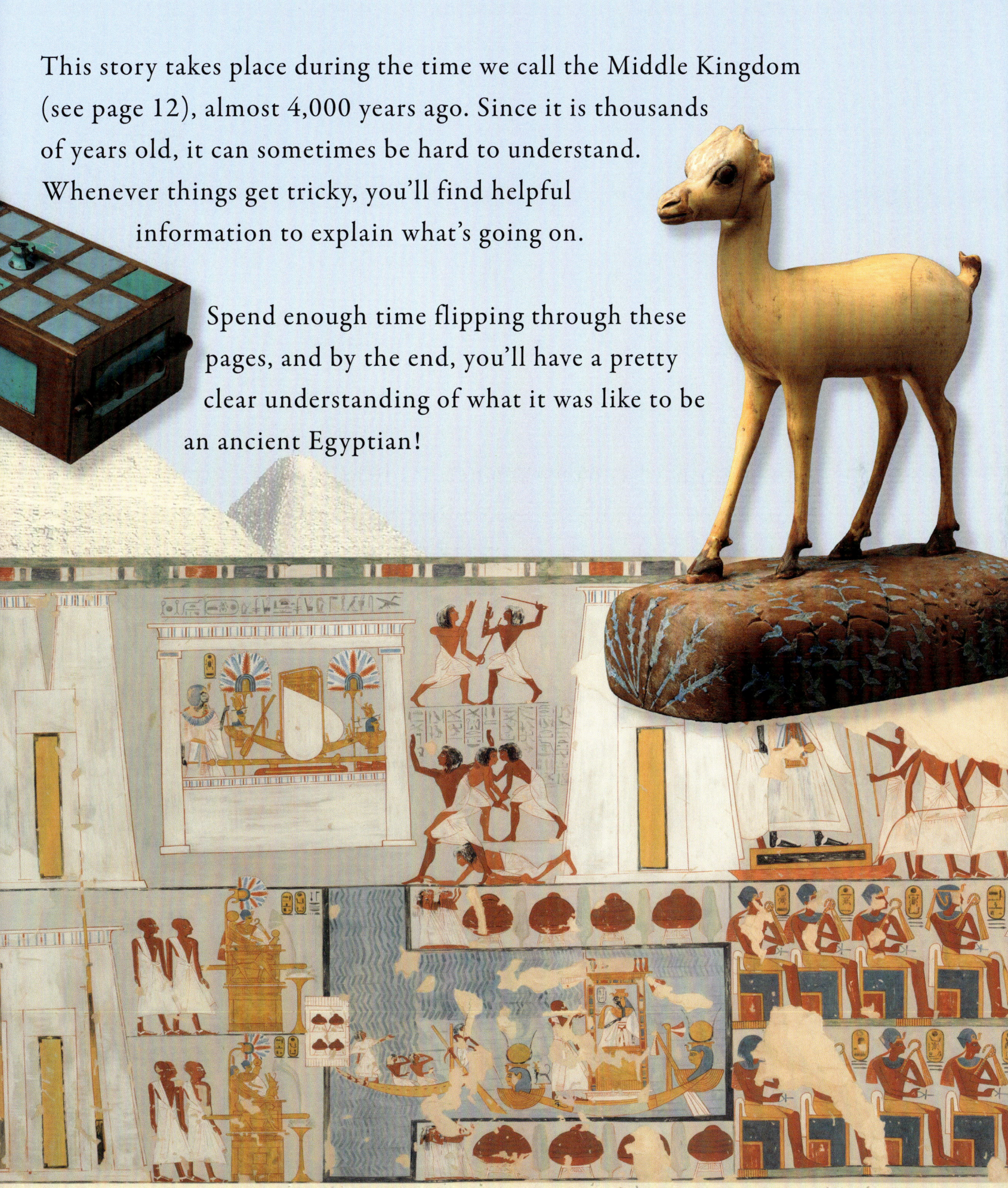

# Ready to Learn Some Ancient Egyptian?

Throughout this book, you will learn some ancient Egyptian words. They'll be written in hieroglyphs and in two other ways: transliteration (the way Egyptologists spell out the sounds of the Egyptian language) and with a guide to the sounds of the words, to help you read them aloud. You'll also learn the meaning in English. Here's an example:

*kmt* (say: ke•met) "Egypt"

You can practice saying this word and the others in this book, and impress your friends with your new vocabulary!

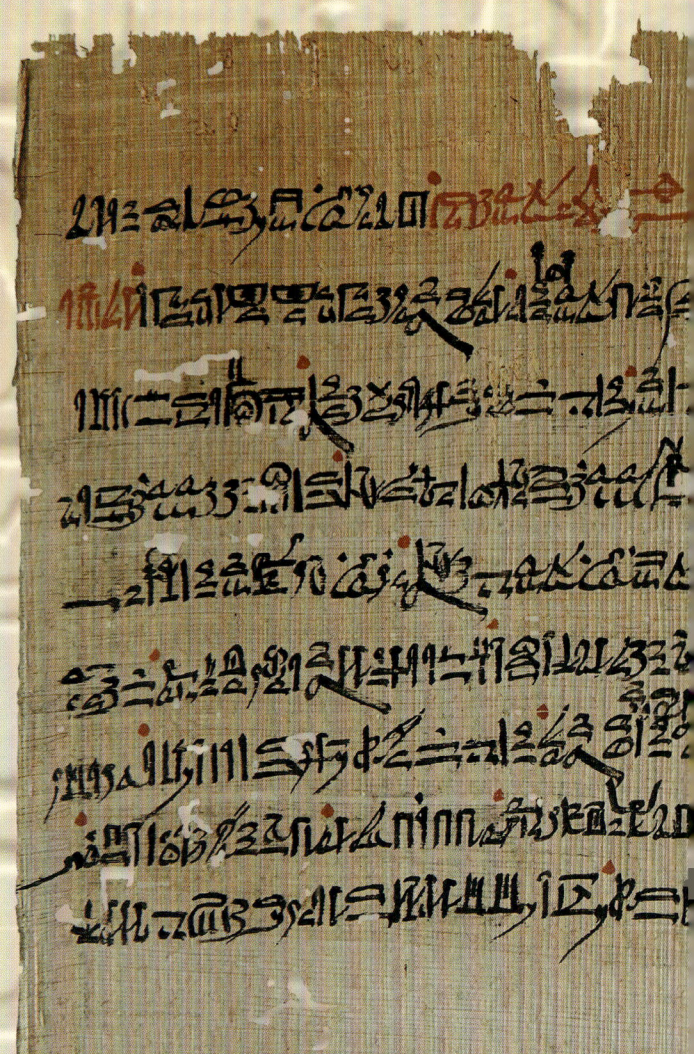

## What are hieroglyphs?

To the ancient Egyptians, hieroglyphs were known as *mdw nṯr* (say: med•oo net•cher) "sacred writing." The word "hieroglyph" comes from the ancient Greek translation of this Egyptian phrase: in ancient Greek, "hiero" means "sacred" and "glyph" means "writing."

# Hieroglyphs only represent consonants

Many people think that hieroglyphs are "picture writing," but that's not the whole story. For example, a hieroglyph such as 🐦 can mean "bird," but it usually doesn't. While many hieroglyphs look like real-world objects and creatures, most often they represent sounds, just like the letters of the English alphabet. But unlike writing in English, hieroglyphs represent the sounds of the ancient Egyptian language.

Papyrus Sallier contains the only complete copy of this story. It was written with ink on papyrus using a writing system known as hieratic.

There were vowels in the ancient Egyptian language, but hieroglyphs only represent consonants. They leave out all the vowels. Egyptologists don't always know what the real vowels were, so they add in the letter "e" between consonants to make Egyptian words easier for people today to pronounce. For example, the ancient Egyptian word for Egypt is 𓆎𓅓𓏏𓊖. Egyptologists spell out (transliterate) this word as *kmt*, and pronounce it ke•met, adding e's between the consonants to make it easier to say.

Some hieroglyphs represent single sounds, just like the letters of the English alphabet, while others represent multiple sounds, such as ⊗ *niwt* (say: nee•oot) "town" and 𓅓𓆷 *ꜥš3* (say: a•sha) "many." But aren't the "a" sounds in 𓅓𓆷, and the "ee" and "oo" sounds in ⊗, vowels? In fact, these were consonants in ancient Egyptian, but Egyptologists pronounce them like English vowels! All sounds represented by hieroglyphs are actually consonants. Remember, the original Egyptian vowels are not written in hieroglyphs.

## Hieroglyphs work in three ways

As you've already learned, hieroglyphs usually represent sounds. For example, ⎯, the hieroglyph of an arm, makes the English sound "a". However, hieroglyphs also work in two other ways:

In some cases, they represent entire words: ⎯ᶜ (say: a) "arm." And in other cases, they come at the very end of a word, to show the idea of that word: 𓀜⎯ *ḥwi* (say: hoo•ee) "hit"—because you hit something with your arm. You'll see hieroglyphs used in all three ways throughout this book.

## Handwritten hieroglyphs?

Try to copy down the ancient Egyptian word for Egypt: 𓆑⊗. How long did it take you? Is it easier or more difficult to write the English word "Egypt"? Writing even a single word in hieroglyphs is time consuming. Imagine if you were a scribe and had to fill an entire page! Ancient Egyptians had the same problem: it takes way too long to write

10

hieroglyphs. They solved this by creating a system of handwritten hieroglyphs that made it easier to write, which we call hieratic. The original version of this story was written on papyrus, in hieratic.

Egyptian scribes usually wrote in black ink, but they used red ink at the start of paragraphs and for other important sentences. As you read the translation of this story, spot which words the ancient scribe chose to write in red on the original papyrus.

You now have a better understanding of hieroglyphs! This book won't teach you everything about the Egyptian language, so if you want to learn more, check out *Reading Egyptian Art: A Hieroglyphic Guide to Ancient Egyptian Painting and Sculpture* by Richard Wilkinson.

# Timeline

**Earliest Hieroglyphic Inscription**
The first hieroglyphs appear on small ivory tags found in Tomb U-j at Abydos.

**Unification**
Menes (Narmer) unites Upper and Lower Egypt.

**The Great Pyramid**
King Khufu is buried in his famous tomb.

**Book of the Dead**
The earliest versions of the "Book of the Dead" are written around this time.

**Re-unification**
Mentuhotep II reunites Egypt, beginning the Middle Kingdom.

**Re-re-unification**
Ahmose I expels the Hyksos and declares the beginning of the New Kingdom.

**Oldest Texts**
The oldest copies of this story are written.

**Reign of Hatshepsut**
Egypt's most famous female king ruled at this time.

**Complete Copy**
Papyrus Sallier, the only complete copy of this story, was written during the New Kingdom.

**Copies of Copies...**
Most copies of this story come from the Third Intermediate Period. They are written on small pieces of stone called ostraca.

3000 BCE — Archaic Period
2500 BCE — Old Kingdom
First Intermediate Period
2000 BCE — Middle Kingdom
Second Intermediate Period
1500 BCE — New Kingdom
1000 BCE — Third Intermediate Period
Late Period
500 BCE — Hellenistic Period

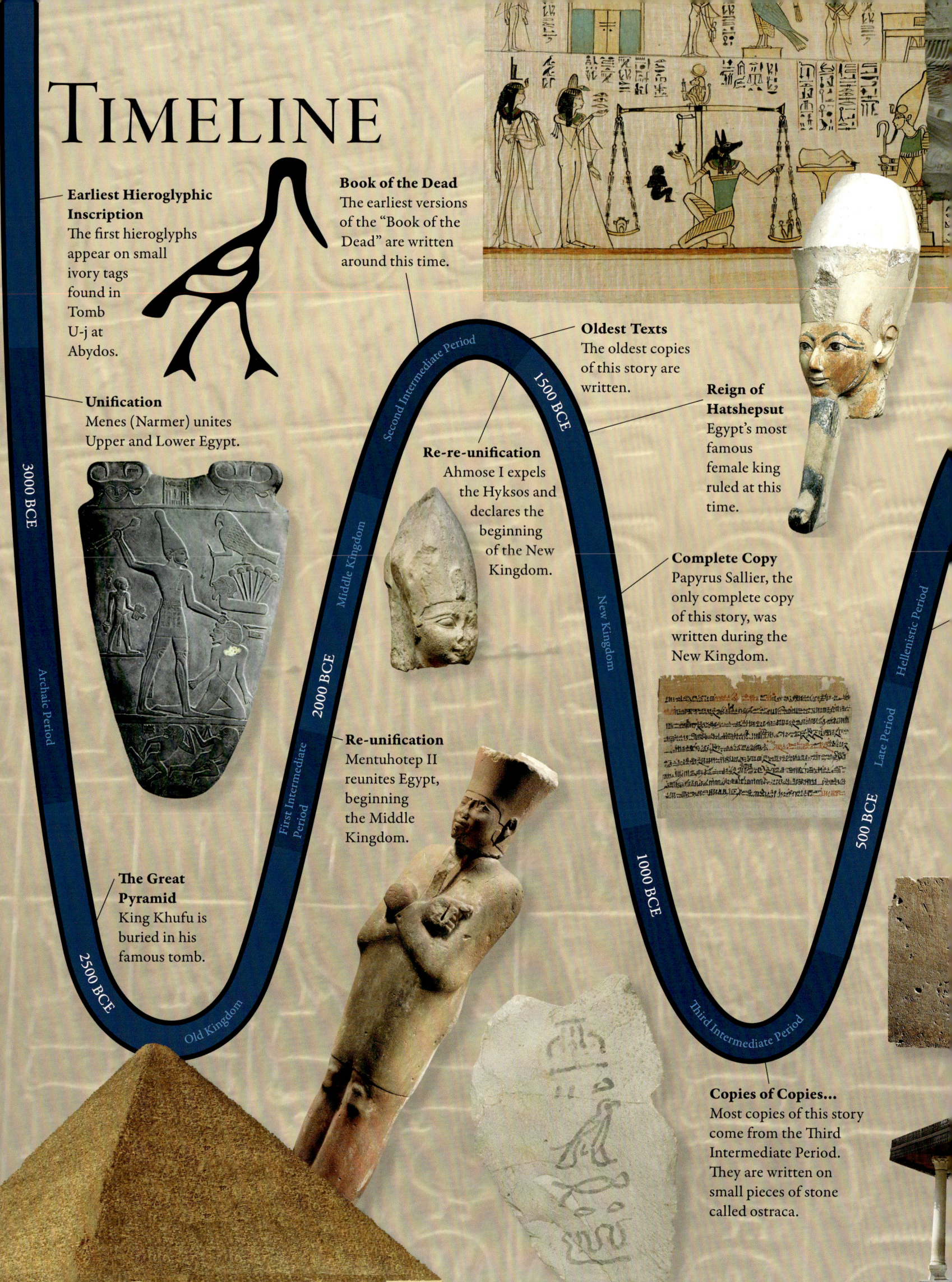

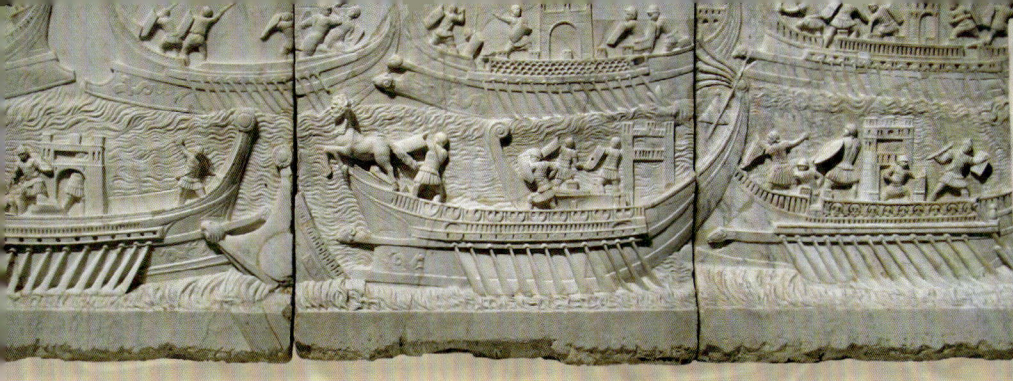

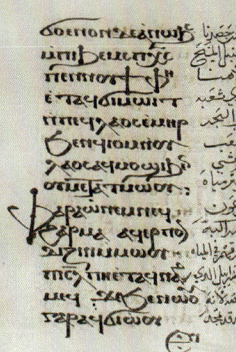

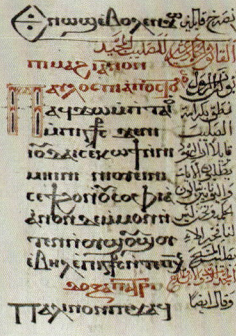

**Battle of Actium**
Roman forces led by Octavian defeat Cleopatra and Marc Antony's army, making Egypt a Roman province.

**Last Egyptian Queen**
The famous Cleopatra lived closer in time to us than she did to the building of the Great Pyramid. Check this timeline to see for yourself!

Year 0

Roman Period

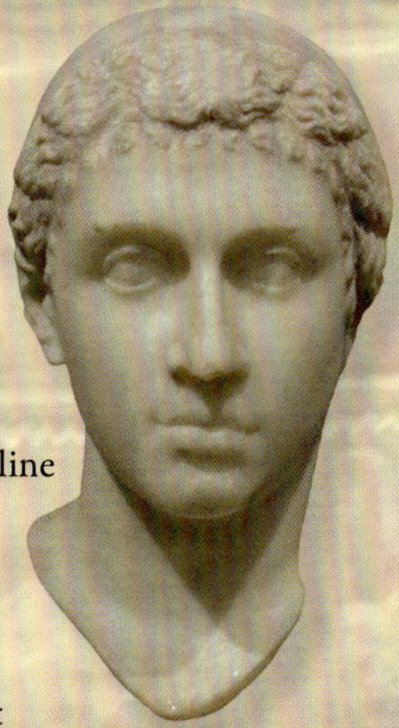

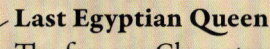

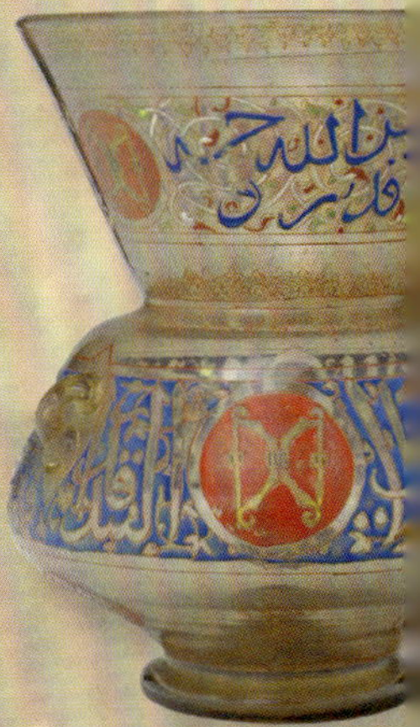

**Christian Era**
Christianity begins to spread to Egypt. It would eventually become the dominant religion, replacing the ancient Egyptian religion entirely.

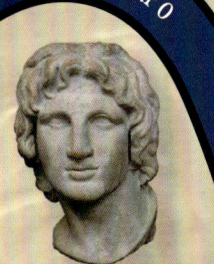

**Greeks in Egypt**
Alexander the Great conquers Egypt, beginning the Hellenistic Period, a time when Greeks ruled over Egypt.

Byzantine Period

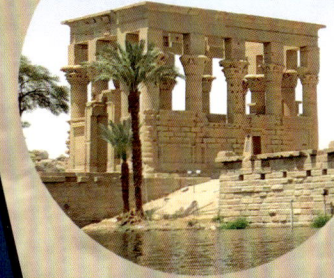

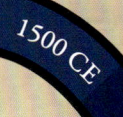

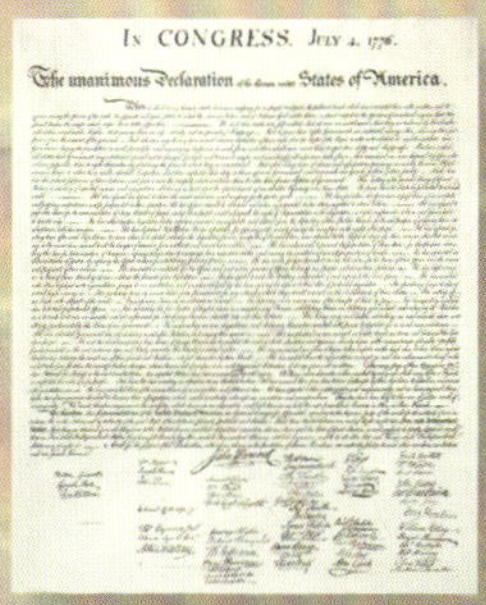

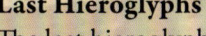

**Last Hieroglyphs**
The last hieroglyphic inscription is carved on the temple of Philae in Upper Egypt.

500 CE

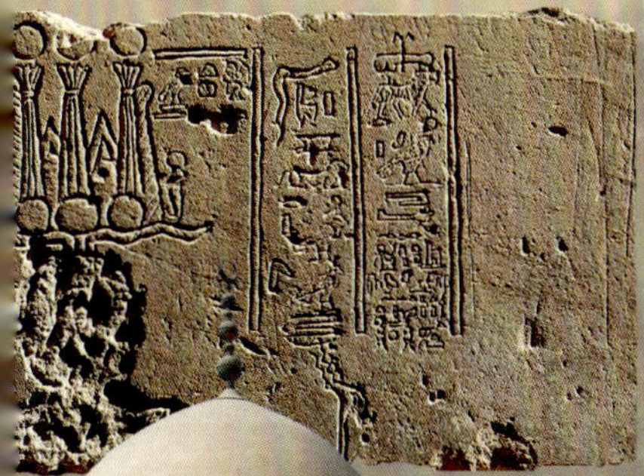

**Last Temple**
The last functioning Egyptian temple, Philae, is closed by order of the Byzantine emperor Justinian.

Islamic Period

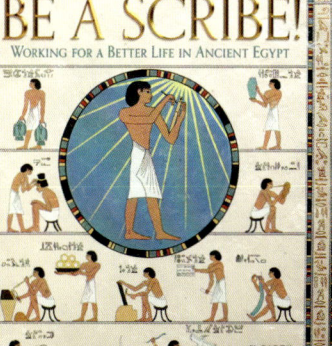

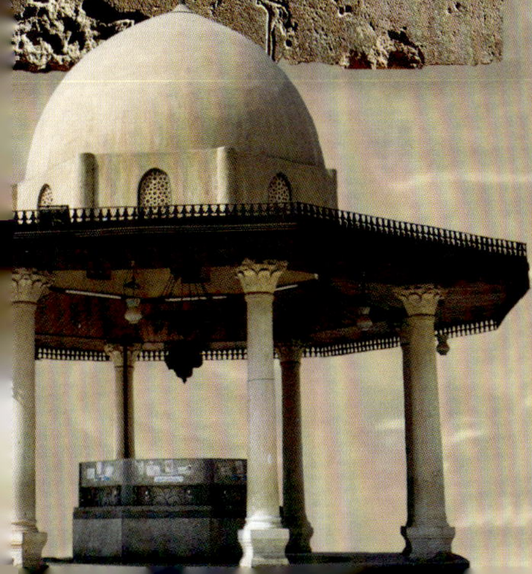

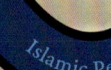

**Arab Conquest**
Muslim Arabs, led by Amr ibn al-As, conquer Egypt and set up an Islamic government.

1000 CE

1500 CE

**Coptic to Arabic**
Gradually, Coptic—the last form of the ancient Egyptian language—was supplanted by Arabic as the language of the Egyptians. Books from the medieval period use both languages side by side.

Ottoman Empire

**Birth of the USA**
The Declaration of Independence is signed. Notice how recent this famous historical event is compared to the long history of Egypt.

European Colonialism

2000 CE

Arab Republic of Egypt

***Be a Scribe!***
The book you're reading right now hits the shelves.

Canaan

Wood in Egypt usually came from Lebanon— the land of the *Aamu*.

Sinai

There were many turquoise mines in the Sinai.

Mediterranean Sea

Great Bitter Lake

⊗ Pelisium
⊗ Sile
⊗ Damietta
⊗ Avaris
⊗ Bubastis
⊗ Busiris
⊗ Heliopolis
⊗ Buto
⊗ Naukratis
⊗ Alexandria
Delta Marshes
⊗ Memphis
⊗ Itjtawy
⊗ Lahun
⊗ Herakleopolis
Faiyum Oasis
⊗ Crocodilopolis

Lower Egypt

# Journey

# ON THE RIVER

"**This is the beginning of the teaching** which Khety, son of Duauf and a man from Sile, made for his son Pepi. They were traveling upstream to the capital to enroll Pepi in the classroom of the scribes among the children of the most important officials."

*This wooden boat model shows what traveling by ship upstream on the Nile might have looked like.*

*A cabin on the deck provides shade and a place to store valuables.*

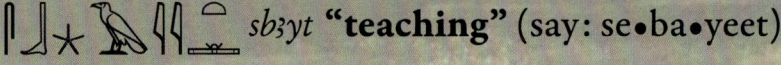 *sbꜣyt* **"teaching"** (say: se•ba•yeet)

This word normally appears at the beginning of wisdom texts like this one. Wisdom texts are collections of advice and popular sayings that instruct people about how to act properly. Although *Be a Scribe!* tells us about the many different jobs in ancient Egypt, it also teaches readers how to live their lives.

**Where is Sile?**
Sile (say: see•lay) was a remote desert town east of the Nile Delta. This town was far away from the major cities of ancient Egypt. To see where it was, look at the map on page 14. Or see the small map to the right.

*zḫꜣ* **"scribe"** (say: ze•kha)

"Scribe" is the name for a variety of related jobs in ancient Egypt, all of which centered on writing. In those days, most people did not know how to read or write, so writing was a highly desired skill. A scribe would have to study from a young age in order to learn all of the different hieroglyphs and become proficient in writing ancient Egyptian. Once he completed his training, he could write important documents and even work in the service of the king.

# Where was the capital of ancient Egypt?

The capital of ancient Egypt changed many times over the course of its history. Since most Egyptologists believe that the events in *Be a Scribe!* are supposed to take place in the Middle Kingdom, "the capital" could be one of two places: Thebes, the capital during the 11th Dynasty, or Itjtawy, the capital during the 12th Dynasty. Both places were located upstream of Sile.

A man at the bow keeps a close watch on the river's depth.

A model of an ancient Egyptian official

Oarsmen propel the boat when the wind or the river's current isn't enough.

*ḫnty* **"to travel upstream"** (say: khen•tee)

The Nile River flows from south to north, so when you're traveling upstream, it means that you're going south. And if you're traveling downstream, it means you're going north. If you look at the map on page 14, you'll notice that the area called Upper Egypt is south of the area called Lower Egypt. This is because Upper Egypt is farther upstream and Lower Egypt is farther downstream.

This prehistoric painted vase from more than 5,000 years ago shows how important boats were to the Egyptians from the very beginning. The Nile was the main means of travel for all of Egypt.

# Fatherly Advice

"**Then Khety said to his son,** I have seen many beatings, so you should set your heart to writing. I have seen a man rescued from his labor by becoming a scribe; there is nothing better than writing! It is a safe decision. At the end of *Kemyt* you will find this sentence: 'If the scribe resides in the capital, he'll never be poor.' If he does what others need, then he will always be busy."

A tomb scene showing a public beating

### "I have seen many beatings"
Physical punishment was common in ancient Egypt. Anything from failing to pay your taxes to petty theft could be punished by beating. But unlike in our time, people weren't imprisoned very often. Instead, punishments were carried out right then and there and could be very harsh. Khety tells his son that he has "seen many beatings" in order to encourage him to become a scribe. Scribes, he suggests, were less likely to be beaten than other people, perhaps because they were treated with more respect than the average person.

Heart scarabs—stones or other materials carved into the shape of scarab beetles— were placed above the hearts of mummified people to protect this organ in the afterlife.

𓄣 *ib* **"heart"** (say: eeb)

Even though this word is written with the hieroglyph for "heart," it also means "mind." The ancient Egyptians believed that the brain was useless and that the heart did all of the thinking. When a person was mummified, the heart was left inside the body while the brain was thrown away.

A heart-shaped amulet was thought to protect its wearer from harm.

See how it looks like the hieroglyph for heart!

**"It is a safe decision."**
Literally, the original ancient Egyptian sentence says, "It is like something upon the water." The "something" on the water probably refers to boats, which were an important part of Egyptian life. Just as a boat can keep you afloat, Khety feels that being a scribe is "a safe decision" that can help you in times of crisis.

**What is *Kemyt*?**
*Kemyt* is an ancient Egyptian wisdom text that every aspiring scribe had to copy when they were learning to write. It is a standard collection of wise sayings, which were thought to provide good advice to young people. In this way, it was a lot like the story you're reading right now!

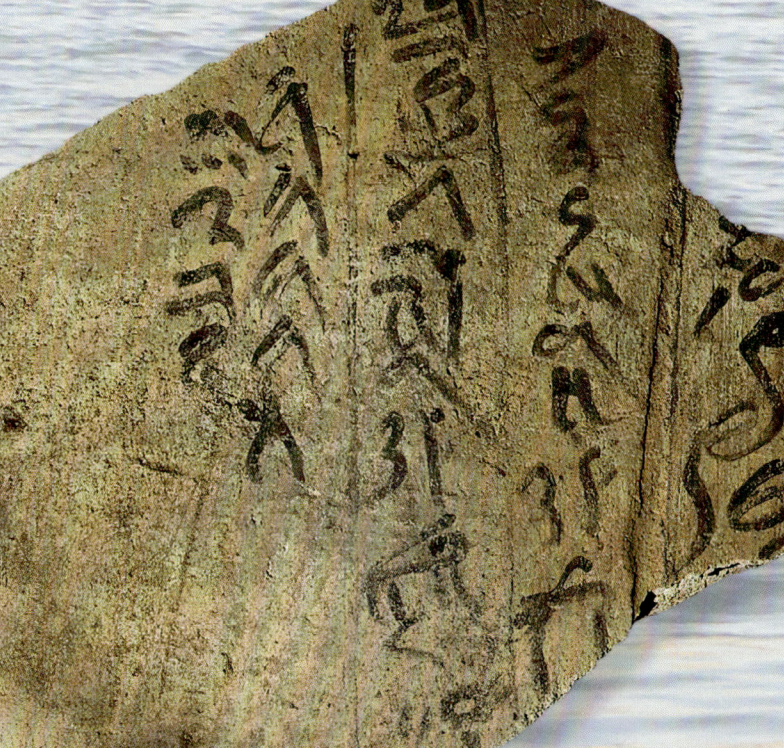

This small part of a letter in the style of *Kemyt* is written on an ostracon, a piece of pottery used in ancient times for everyday writing—kind of like the sticky notes of the ancient world.

# The Best Job

**"I've never seen a job like being a scribe!** By telling you about it, I'll make you love writing more than your mother. I'll show you what a good salary is like. Being a scribe is great, it's better than every other job. It's like nothing on earth. Fortune starts for him when he is only a child, people already seek advice from him. He is sent to run errands, and before he comes back he puts on a kilt."

This wooden granary model shows scribes at work tallying up the amount of grain the workers are processing.

Scribes had many tasks other than writing, including making architectural drawings like this one!

### "he puts on a kilt"
Ancient Egyptian men with high status often wore kilts. While most Egyptian children wore simple loincloths, children who were training to be scribes began to wear kilts from a young age. Wearing a kilt in ancient Egypt would be like wearing a suit in modern times—it was an unusual item of clothing for younger people.

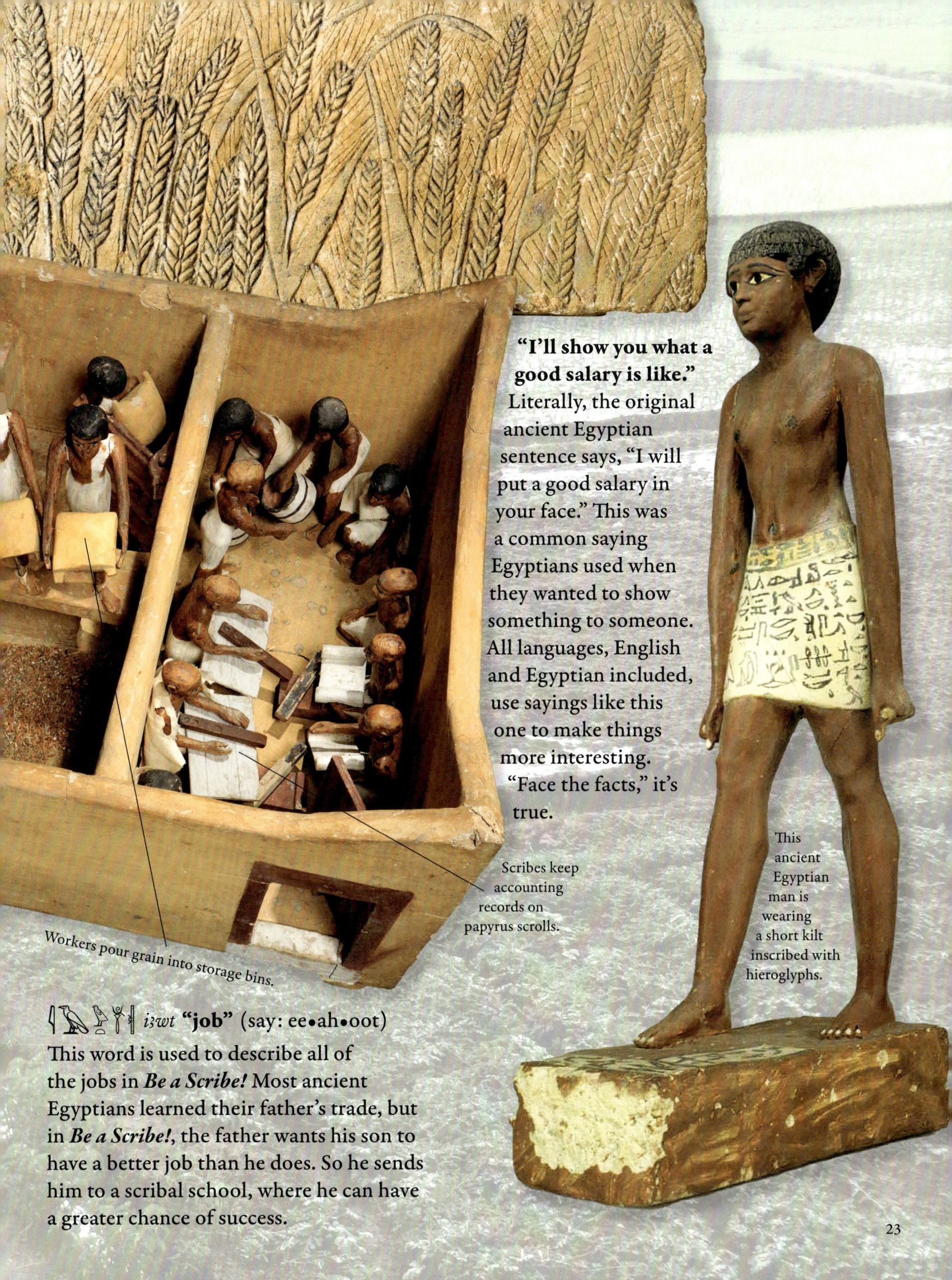

"**I'll show you what a good salary is like.**" Literally, the original ancient Egyptian sentence says, "I will put a good salary in your face." This was a common saying Egyptians used when they wanted to show something to someone. All languages, English and Egyptian included, use sayings like this one to make things more interesting. "Face the facts," it's true.

Scribes keep accounting records on papyrus scrolls.

Workers pour grain into storage bins.

This ancient Egyptian man is wearing a short kilt inscribed with hieroglyphs.

i3wt **"job"** (say: ee•ah•oot)
This word is used to describe all of the jobs in *Be a Scribe!* Most ancient Egyptians learned their father's trade, but in *Be a Scribe!*, the father wants his son to have a better job than he does. So he sends him to a scribal school, where he can have a greater chance of success.

# JOBS

# The Smith

"**I've never watched a sculptor** or a goldsmith do their work, but I have watched a coppersmith at the mouth of his forge. He has fingers like those of crocodiles, and is stinkier than an egg or a fish."

This tomb scene shows sculptors working on a statue.

This gold ring made for the priest Sienamun shows the skill of Egyptian metalworkers.

𓎟𓃀𓏭 *gnwty* **"sculptor"** (say: ge•noo•tee)

𓎟𓃀𓏭 *nby* **"goldsmith"** (say: neb•ee)

𓎟𓃀𓏭 *ḥmty* **"coppersmith"** (say: hem•tee)

Ancient Egyptian sculptors and smiths weren't artists in the modern sense. They were skilled craftsmen who had to work within a set of artistic traditions dating back thousands of years. There was little room for creativity. While they weren't praised for their uniqueness, they were recognized for their skill and ability.

This tomb scene shows metalworkers pouring metal from a crucible into a large mold.

ḫryt **"forge"** (say: her•eet)

A forge is like an oven, except it's used to heat and shape metals instead of food. A worker would melt a piece of copper or gold inside a crucible (a ceramic cup used for holding molten metal) and then pour it into a pre-made mold. After some time the metal would harden into that shape and could be taken out of the mold.

This tomb scene shows a man using a forge to melt metal. He blows on the forge with a pipe to increase the oxygen inside and make it hotter.

This ceramic crucible was used to pour molten metal into molds.

Egyptian metalsmiths made many kinds of objects out of bronze (a mixture of copper and tin), such as this cat statue and fish pendant.

**"He has fingers like those of crocodiles"**
Crocodiles have rough, scaly fingers, just like metalworkers, whose hands become dry from hours spent working with molten metal and toxic chemicals. But a scribe, who didn't do that kind of work with his hands, would not have "crocodile fingers."

# The Carpenter

"**When a carpenter uses an adze,** he becomes more tired than a farmer. The carpenter's 'field' is made of wood, and his tools are made of copper. Only the night can rescue him when he has done more than his two arms can handle—but he still has to light a lamp."

A tomb scene showing a carpenter using an adze

*ḥmw* **"carpenter"** (say: hem•oo) Egyptian carpenters worked with wood to make objects such as statues, furniture, and coffins. The hieroglyph for "carpenter" (first in the word above) is a picture of the kind of drill they used in their work.

This tomb scene shows a variety of craftsmen making objects that would be buried in a person's tomb.

ḫt **"wood"** (say: khet)

Although there are many trees in Egypt, their wood isn't the best for carpentry. Most of the wood used to make high-quality objects was imported from the area that is now Lebanon. If a carpenter was using local Egyptian wood to make a large object, they might have to fit together oddly shaped pieces, almost like a puzzle.

ꜥnt **"adze"** (say: ah•net)

An adze is a tool that is used to carve, smooth, or strip the bark from wood. The word for adze in Egyptian is also the word for fingernail, because fingernails can be used for similar purposes: they can also scoop and scratch things away.

This is a real ancient Egyptian adze! Notice its similarity to the fourth hieroglyph from the left.

This lamp would have been filled with oil and has a hole to allow for a wick.

**"he still has to light a lamp"**

Although the workday for many ancient Egyptians ended at sunset, according to Khety, carpenters often labored well into the night. If you had to work after dark, then you would need to use a lamp. Remember, there was no electricity!

# The Jeweler

**"The jeweler searches every hard ore with a chisel.** By the time he puts in all of the inlays, his arms are ruined, and he is exhausted. He sits on a pile of the food of Re, but his knees and spine are bent."

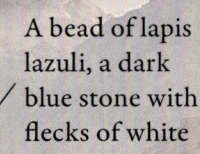

A jewelry box

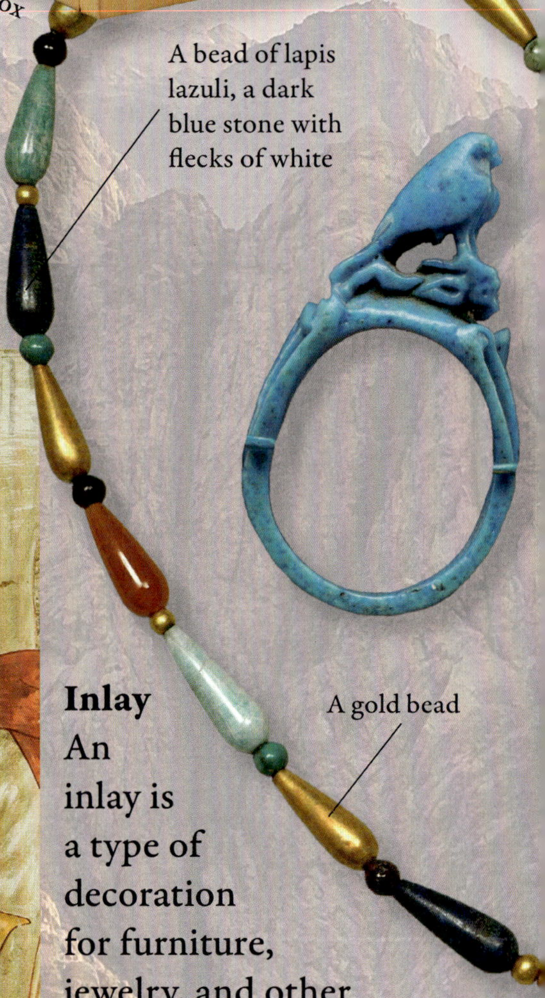

A bead of lapis lazuli, a dark blue stone with flecks of white

A gold bead

**Inlay**
An inlay is a type of decoration for furniture, jewelry, and other objects. Inlays are "laid in": jewelers insert pieces of precious material into the surface of an object to create colorful patterns. In ancient Egypt, jewelers would make a small hole in the object they were crafting and fill the hole with a precious stone or gem, cut to a precise fit.

A gold figurine of Amun showcases the skill of Egyptian craftworkers.

The tomb scene above shows foreign people bringing tribute, including jewelry.

30

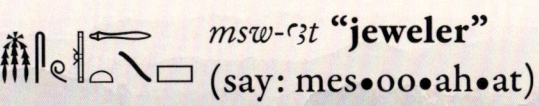 *ꜣt* **"ore"** (say: ah•at)

An ore is a piece of stone that contains metals, such as gold or copper, or gemstones, such as turquoise or lapis lazuli. Miners extract ores from the land and jewelers process them into gems, lumps of raw metal called ingots, or expensive items containing precious materials.

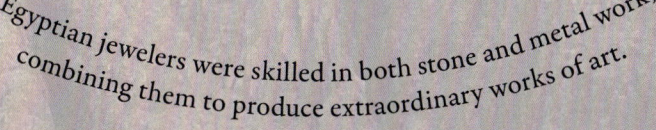 *msw-ꜣt* **"jeweler"** (say: mes•oo•ah•at)

Being a jeweler in ancient Egypt meant you had one of two important tasks. Some jewelers extracted valuable materials from stones and ores, while others carved and cut the resulting gems to make luxury items such as necklaces and jewelry boxes. Literally, this Egyptian word means "birther of ore"—the idea being that the raw stone was "pregnant" with valuable materials.

Egyptian jewelers were skilled in both stone and metal work, combining them to produce extraordinary works of art.

A bead made from carnelian, a red semiprecious stone

A bead of turquoise, a light blue stone

The name of the king Senwosret II

**"the food of Re"**

This phrase refers to gold. Gold is associated with the gods in ancient Egypt, especially with solar gods such as Re—think about the similarities between the color and shine of gold and sunlight. Although the jeweler "sits on a pile" of gold, he doesn't get to keep it, and worse, his body is worn out because of the work!

This man strings beads onto a necklace.    This man uses a bow to drill beads.

31

# The Barber

"**The barber shaves until the end of the night.** He puts the razor on the neck and then puts it on his elbow. He goes from street to street to find someone to shave. He will exhaust his two arms in order to fill his stomach, like a bee working to eat."

A jar for eye paint with an applicator stick

A bronze razor

Tweezers

A bronze mirror

A whetstone

A cosmetic set, which belonged to an ancient Egyptian woman

ḥ⸗q "**barber**" (say: khak) In Egyptian, the words for barber and shave are the same. The last hieroglyph in the word for barber is a picture of the kind of razor they used in their work. Egyptian barbers traveled around searching for customers instead of working in a shop—that's why the barber in *Be a Scribe!* "goes from street to street."

Egyptian children often wore a sidelock—a single braid on one side of the head.

A razor like the one in the hieroglyph, which belonged to a woman named Hatnefer

This is the burial mask of Hatnefer, the woman who owned the razor above.

32

## Who went to the barber in ancient Egypt?

Everyone! At various times in Egyptian history, all sorts of people shaved their heads and wore wigs. (Notice that the shaving tools on these pages belonged to women.) Certain kinds of priests always shaved their heads and bodies as a way of staying clean and pure to enter the temple, while children's heads were shaved except for one lock of hair on the side.

### "He puts the razor on the neck and then puts it on his elbow"

Barbers always have to work with a clean blade to avoid cutting their customers. After shaving a customer's neck, the barber would wipe the razor on his elbow and then repeat this motion over and over again. This constant repetition might make the job seem dull and exhausting.

A tomb scene depicting the ancient Egyptian equivalent of a barbershop—many people wait for the barber to cut their hair.

Certain kinds of priests shaved off all their hair because hair was thought to be ritually impure.

### "like a bee working to eat"

In English, a "busy bee" is someone who is always working. Ancient Egyptians used a similar metaphor. Khety suggests that the barber in *Be a Scribe!* can't take a day off work unless he's fine with skipping a meal. His income is so low that he is unable to save his earnings from one day to the next.

# The Trader

"**The trader travels downstream to the Delta marshes** to make a profit for himself. He has done more than his two arms can handle. The mosquitoes have killed him, the fleas have bitten him. He has been bitten, and so he is punished."

A tomb scene showing a marsh with birds and papyrus plants

*bṯty* **"trader"**
(say: be•che•tee)

Literally, this Egyptian word means "runner," since this person would travel swiftly from place to place to do their job. They would buy goods in one place and sell them for profit in another.

This boat has a cabin in the middle to store goods. It has many rowers, perhaps because it is traveling downstream, against the wind.

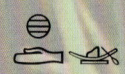 *ḫdy* **"to travel downstream"**
(say: khe•dee)

Remember that the Nile River flows from south to north, so when you're traveling downstream, it means that you're going north. If someone has to go downstream to get to the Delta marshes, it means that they are coming from the south, in Upper Egypt (see the map on page 14).

34

A tomb scene showing a boat being rowed on the Nile

**"He has been bitten, and so he is punished."**
The Nile Delta in Egypt (see the map on page 14) is very watery, and that means there are many mosquitoes and fleas. Not only does the trader's job involve a lot of hard work, but it also takes him to a harsh environment where he is more vulnerable to insects than Egyptians living in other places.

Mosquitoes and other flying insects are annoying pests. Amulets like this one were meant to keep them away.

# The Potter

Egyptian craftspeople could make highly detailed ceramic figures.

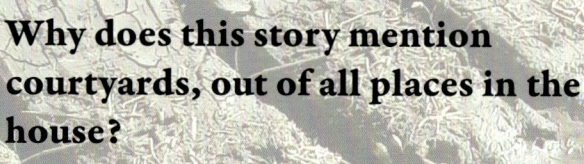

"**The common potter is under the earth,** even though he is still alive. He uproots more mud than a pig to fire clay under the ground. His clothing is as hard as a block of stone, and his belt is a rag. The hot air comes out from the fire and enters forcefully into his nose. He has to knead the clay himself—he stomps on it with his two feet. He is turned away from the courtyard of every house because he is covered in mud."

Egyptian potters didn't only make pots: they could make all kinds of things, including this model of a house.

**Why does this story mention courtyards, out of all places in the house?**
Courtyards were an important part of ancient Egyptian houses. Most houses had both indoor spaces and an enclosed outdoor courtyard. Unlike the other parts of the house, which were more private, courtyards were places where guests could visit—unless they were unwelcome, like the potter in *Be a Scribe!*

A typical ancient Egyptian storage jar: simple and practical

This model shows a potter making a pot using a wheel.

Sometimes potters decided to get creative, as in the case of the two feet supporting this bowl.

In some periods of Egyptian history, pots with painted decorations were in style, as in the case of this water flask.

𓇋𓈎𓂧𓅱𓀀 *iqdw* "**potter**" (say: ee•ked•oo)

Pottery—baked clay containers—was made in ancient Egypt from at least 5200 BCE. Egyptian potters worked clay with their hands or on a pottery wheel. They formed the clay into cooking pots, jars for storage and transport, dishes for eating and drinking, and even molds for shaping bread. Once the clay was shaped, they baked it in a special oven called a kiln, which created the extreme heat needed to make solid, watertight containers. Kilns were often built below ground ("under the earth").

# The Wall Builder

**"I will speak to you about how it is to be a wall builder.** His body is chapped because he has to build outside in sandstorms wearing only a loincloth, a belt of braided thread high up his waist. His two arms are robbed of their strength, they are mixed with all his filth. He eats bread with his fingers, but he only washes himself once a day."

A man makes bricks from the kneaded mud using a mold.

A man digs up earth to be made into bricks.

A man kneads mud with his feet.

A man carries kneaded mud to the brick maker.

*iqdw inbw* **"wall builder"** (say: ee•ked•oo een•boo)
Notice that this job contains one of the same words as "potter" in the previous section. In fact, they describe similar jobs: both build things out of mud. While the potter used it to make containers, the builder used it to make mudbricks. Potters baked clay in kilns, but builders baked mudbricks in the heat of the sun.

## What are these walls for?

You might associate ancient Egyptian buildings with stone because most of the remaining temples and tombs are made out of stone. However, ancient Egyptians themselves lived in houses made of mudbrick. Even the king lived in a palace with mudbrick walls. Wall builders had a very important job because every new construction project started with them.

A model of a two-story house. A real house of this sort would have been built out of mudbrick.

A brick mold like the one used in the tomb scene on the left

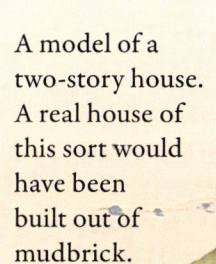

## Why use mudbrick?

Mudbrick might sound like a low-quality building material, but in fact it was well suited to the Egyptian environment. Mudbrick was easy to make from the materials ancient Egyptians had around them. It is good at protecting against the heat of the sun, and it lasts a long time in places where it doesn't rain often. In the hot and dry American Southwest, houses are made out of a similar material called adobe—a word that comes from the Egyptian *dbt* (say: de•bet), meaning "brick."

A mudbrick with the stamp of an official named Senimen

39

# THE ROOFER

**"As for the wall builder, he is more miserable than the roofer in all ways.** The roofs the roofer builds are bigger than 10 × 6 cubits! It takes him longer than a month, after adding all the beams with braided rope and doing all of the other work. He gives his income to his family, providing for his children."

A modern reconstruction from the game Assassin's Creed Origins shows a typical ancient Egyptian house.

*mt* **"roofer"** (say: met)

A wall builder couldn't build a whole house alone. Once he finished the walls of one floor, a roofer would come in with wooden beams, usually made from palm trees. Using a rope and pulley system, the roofer lifted the heavy beams up to the top of the house until they hung over the sides. To add more floors, the wall builder would come back, build the walls of the next floor, and the process would repeat, finishing with the roof. Ancient Egyptian houses could reach three or more stories!

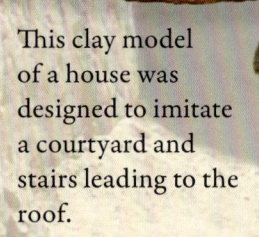

This clay model of a house was designed to imitate a courtyard and stairs leading to the roof.

### "It takes him longer than a month"

Unlike our months, Egyptian months were all exactly 30 days long. If you do the math, that works out to 360 days. What about the other 5? They were added to the end of the year as an extra mini-month. These 5 days were a special time of celebration before the beginning of the new year. Since the Egyptians didn't have a leap year, their calendar crept slowly out of step with the seasons over time.

The hieroglyph for an arm is also used in the word for cubit, because the length of a cubit was about the length of a person's forearm.

This is a cubit stick, marked to measure objects, just like a modern ruler.

The roofs of many ancient Egyptian houses were made out of wood.

### How long is a cubit?

A cubit is a way of measuring length. The length of an Egyptian cubit changed over time. It was based on the length of a person's forearm, but it was also standardized: think about the way a foot refers to a standard length that we all know, even though everyone has a different sized foot. An Egyptian cubit is about 20 inches (50 centimeters) long.

This is an Egyptian measuring stick, with the writing representing fractions of a cubit. Can you see the numbers increasing from right to left?

# The Gardener

"**The gardener is carrying a shoulder-yoke,** and all of his joints are worn out. There is a large lump on his neck, it is producing fluid. He will spend the morning watering the grapevines. At night, he will water the coriander. By noon he is exhausted because of his poor body—but he only gets a chance to rest when he dies. In every aspect it is worse than every job."

These men crush grapes into grape juice with their feet.

These men harvest grapes from the vine.

k3ryw **"gardener"**
(say: ka•ree•oo)

In ancient Egypt, there were no grocery stores—all food had to be produced locally. Gardeners were responsible for growing the fruits and vegetables that people ate every day, so they had a lot of work to do. Grapes were one of the fruits they grew, and the word for gardener contains a hieroglyph of a grapevine (the sixth hieroglyph from the left).

**"He will spend the morning watering the grapevines. At night, he will water the coriander."**
What is the connection between grapevines and coriander (aka cilantro)? When these two plants are grown together in a garden, they benefit each other. Coriander attracts bees that pollinate the grapevines, resulting in more grapes. At the same time, the shade of the grape leaves protects the coriander from the heat of the sun. Egyptian gardeners knew about this relationship and used it to their advantage.

This gardener uses a counterweighted pole with a bucket on the end, called a *shaduf* in Arabic, to lift water from a canal to his plants.

**What is a shoulder-yoke, and why does it hurt the gardener?**
A shoulder-yoke is a wooden beam with two containers, one attached on each end. It allows you to shift the weight of what you're carrying to your back instead of your arms, letting you lift more than you could before. However, it also puts a lot of weight on a person's back and neck. Over time, it can cause lumps and blisters like those Khety describes.

A model from the tomb of a man named Meketre showing a typical Egyptian garden, with fruit trees surrounding a pool of water in the center.

A small model of a shoulder-yoke with two baskets for carrying goods.

# The Tenant Farmer

"**The tenant farmer cries out for eternity** with a voice as loud as a raven's. His fingers have sores on them from constantly rubbing against his tools. He is more tired than a reed-cutter from the Delta marshes, but he is still in rags. He's doing just fine—if being among lions counts as fine! His experience is painful. His corvée labor makes up a third of his income. He has to travel from the marshes all the way to work and only arrives home late in the evening. Walking has worn him out."

In this wooden model, a farmer uses a pair of oxen to plow his field.

ꜥḥwty "**tenant farmer**" (say: ah•hoo•tee)

You probably know what a farmer is, but what about a tenant farmer? In ancient Egypt, most farmers didn't own their own land. Instead, they rented it from a nobleman, who was their landlord, making them his tenants. They agreed to pay rent by giving a portion of their harvest to their landlord. In exchange, they were protected from robbery and other misfortunes. It was a hard job, and they didn't earn much. What's more, if they failed to pay their rent, their landlord might have them beaten.

This harvest scene shows tax collectors measuring the fields and calculating the total grain they produced.

In this tomb scene of people farming, the fields and canals are shown from a bird's-eye view, but the people working in them are seen from the side.

𓉔𓄿𓄿𓏏𓈅 *ḥꜣwt* **"corvée labor"** (say: ha•oot)
Corvée (say: cor•vay) labor is a system where the government requires people to do unpaid work for the state instead of paying taxes. Ancient Egyptian corvée labor created a workforce for projects such as irrigation canals and roads, and even monuments such as the pyramids.

**"He is more tired than a reed-cutter from the Delta marshes"**
This is now the second time that *Be a Scribe!* has mentioned the Delta marshes. Reed-cutters were known to have been doing hard work, as this line shows, so it is interesting that the reed-cutter never gets a full section of his own in this entire story. Perhaps Khety and his son were familiar enough with this job that it didn't need much explanation. Or maybe there is a different reason. Why do you think it might be missing?

45

# The Weaver

**"The weaver is inside the weaving-room. He is worse off than a woman. His knees are pressed against his stomach, and he is unable to breathe. If he wastes a day not weaving, he is beaten with fifty lashes. He gives some bread to the doorkeeper just to let him see daylight."**

*qnwy* **"weaver"** (say: ken•wee) The clothes that you are wearing right now were probably made on a mechanical loom—a machine that automatically weaves fabric from thread. This machine did not exist in ancient Egypt, so clothing had to be woven by hand. Egyptian weavers, who were often women, worked for many hours to produce a single piece of fabric. Today, that same piece of fabric could be made in just a few seconds.

These wooden objects are called shuttles. They were used to pull thread on a loom in order to make fabric.

In this wooden model of a weaving room, the woman in the back uses a shuttle to weave the horizontal threads under and over the vertical ones.

Ancient linen fabric with a fringe of linen thread at the bottom. It's almost 3,000 years old!

**"The weaver is inside the weaving-room. He is worse off than a woman."**
This might sound like an insult to women, but it actually tells us a lot about the kind of work women did in ancient Egypt. You may have noticed that in Egyptian art, men are shown with reddish-brown skin, and women with yellow skin. This difference is an artistic choice to show that men spent more time working outside in the sun than women did. A man who worked as a weaver would not only have to do the hard job of weaving, but he would also have to spend all of his time indoors—something that seems to have been undesirable.

In this tomb scene, an overseer watches over the weavers as they work. The man at the far right uses a drop spindle to spin thread.

ꜥqw **"bread"** (say: ah•koo)

Originally, this ancient Egyptian word meant "income." At the time when *Be a Scribe!* takes place, most Egyptians were paid in grain. Eventually, people associated income with bread, and this word took on a double meaning. Just like some people do today, ancient Egyptians sometimes said "bread" when they really meant "money."

**"He gives some bread to the doorkeeper just to let him see daylight."**
*Be a Scribe!* makes it clear that a working Egyptian man did not want to be stuck inside all the time. The weaver here is dying to escape from the room that he works in, but the only way to get out into the fresh air is to bribe the doorman. He does so by giving the doorman some of his income—maybe just a piece of bread!

# The Weapon Maker

**"The weapon maker is utterly lost whenever he goes out to the outskirts.** He pays more for his donkeys than what their work can repay him. He has to pay the locals in order to find his way. He will go home and arrive at his house in the evening. Walking has worn him out."

This model of a shield and quiver with spears shows the typical Egyptian cowhide covering.

*irw ꜥḥꜣw* **"weapon maker"** (say: ee•roo a•ha•oo) Literally, the ancient Egyptian for this word means "maker of weapons." But what sort of weapons? The Egyptian word includes a hieroglyph that indicates that those weapons were made of wood. (It's the one that looks like a stick.) Other clues in this section hint at what sort of wood the weapon maker might have been using. Trees such as acacia, tamarisk, and sycomore provided wood for small-scale objects, such as the handles of weapons.

This bow, made from a single piece of wood, is about three feet (one meter) in length.

𓈉 *ḫ₃st* **"outskirts"** (say: kha•set)

This word is especially difficult to translate into English. It was used to describe many different landscapes, including those outside of Egypt. The first hieroglyph above shows three hills, which gives us a clue about what sort of place this word describes. It can refer to the deserts east and west of the Nile, or the hilly areas to the northeast. Based on the information from this section, the area that the weapon maker travels to must be close enough that he can walk there and back within a day, but far enough that he easily gets lost. Although it is far from his home, there are still people who live there and give him directions. Putting it all together, "outskirts" is probably the best translation here.

This battle axe has a strong bronze head and a wooden handle. Notice the knob at the end—this prevents the weapon from slipping out of the wielder's hands.

A bronze sword made around the time this story was written

This javelin has an extremely sharp pointed end, great for piercing the armor of enemies.

**Why does the weapon maker pay more than he earns?**
The weapon maker has to pay for donkeys to carry his goods, and he has to pay the locals in order to know where to go. These costs must be subtracted from any money he earns, making it hard for him to earn a living. This section makes the point that being a weapon maker is not desirable because it is not very profitable.

# The Courier

"**The courier goes out to the outskirts,** after writing a will for his children. He is afraid of lions and *Aamu*. He only feels comfortable when he is in Egypt. He will go home and arrive at his house in the evening. Walking has worn him out. He owns his own estate, but it's made of cloth instead of brick. He comes back unsatisfied."

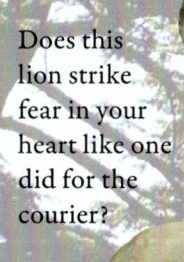

Does this lion strike fear in your heart like one did for the courier?

𓂝𓎛𓀀𓀁 *shhty* **"courier"** (say: se•khekh•tee)

This word comes from another Egyptian word that means "to drag around." Couriers are people who deliver, or drag around, messages or goods. The courier in *Be a Scribe!* is afraid of two dangers on his travels: lions, which really could harm him, and *Aamu*—an Egyptian word used to describe people living in places to the northeast of Egypt. Egyptian stories sometimes describe their foreign neighbors as being more threatening than they actually were. Whatever the hazards, couriers traveled widely throughout the ancient world.

This nearly 4,000-year-old letter was probably delivered by a courier.

Leaders of the *Aamu* bringing goods to Egypt—a trade link that had existed for ages.

This modern tent might be similar to the tent the courier in the story used in his travels 3,000 years ago.

## "He owns his own estate, but it's made of cloth instead of brick."

When you think of an estate, what comes to mind? For the Egyptians, it usually meant a large property, inherited from one generation to the next, that produced goods which were then sold to make a profit for its owners. The owners of these estates were the wealthy elites of ancient Egypt. The courier, too, owns his own estate—but his is a shabby example: just a bunch of cloth tents set up in the desert.

## Is there an echo in here?

Have you noticed something in this section that you've read before? The phrase "walking has worn him out" has appeared twice already. Is Khety running out of bad things to say about these jobs? Do you think they are really as bad as he makes them out to be?

# The Leather Worker

"**The leather worker? His fingers are rotted,** they smell like corpses. His eyes are cast down like those of the poor, he cannot escape his position in society. Because he spends the day cutting strips, he has come to despise clothing."

*stnwy* "**leather worker**" (say: se•ten•wee)

No one knows for sure exactly what job this Egyptian word refers to, but one possibility is a leather worker. What we do know is that this person works with clothing, and he hates it. Whatever he is doing with the clothing makes his fingers smell terrible. So what is he doing? Maybe he works in a tannery, taking raw animal skins and putting them through various chemical processes until they turn into leather. The harsh chemicals used in tanning leather often smell very bad, so a leather worker's fingers would smell like rotten corpses. Gross!

This leather cloak was designed for a priest. The pattern was made to imitate the leopard skins that certain types of Egyptian priests wore.

Ancient Egyptian women often wore long dresses, much like the clothing we wear today.

**"His eyes are cast down like those of the poor"**

When you imagine someone with their eyes cast down, what do you think they are feeling? It could be an emotion like shame or embarrassment. In ancient Egypt, and in the world today, people can sometimes feel that the job they have is a sign of their worth in society. Here, Khety is telling his son that this job is so low class that, if he were to take it, he would feel awful about himself.

## What did ancient Egyptians wear?

Common types of clothing in ancient Egypt included kilts, tunics, and dresses. Kilts were rectangular pieces of fabric draped around the lower half of a person's body. Some kilts came down to the knees, while others were longer, starting around the chest and continuing all the way down to the ankles. Kilts were only worn by men, but tunics could be worn by anyone. Tunics were a type of sleeveless shirt that went all the way to the knees. They could be worn with kilts or dresses. Dresses were worn by women, and could look surprisingly similar to some of the dresses people wear today.

Some ancient Egyptian leather objects have survived to the present day, such as this archer's wrist guard.

This tomb scene shows craftworkers making the leather parts for a new chariot.

This man puts the finishing touches on a leather quiver, which will hold arrows.

This man splits leather to be made into parts for the chariot.

This man adds a strip of leather to a chariot wheel.

This object is the frame of the chariot.

# The Sandal Maker

"**The sandal maker, he is bad in every way.** He will always have too much to do. He's doing just fine—if being among corpses counts as fine! He has to bite leather."

Egyptians made sandals out of many materials—the sandals above are made from leather, while the ones below are made out of woven reeds. Which pair do you think looks more comfortable?

*ṯbw* "**sandal maker**"
(say: che•boo)

An ancient Egyptian's footwear of choice was sandals. Sandals were normally made out of woven reeds, but they could also be made of leather and even gold. Ancient Egyptians wore sandals to protect their feet, but never seem to have worn other kinds of shoes. Why do you think this might be?

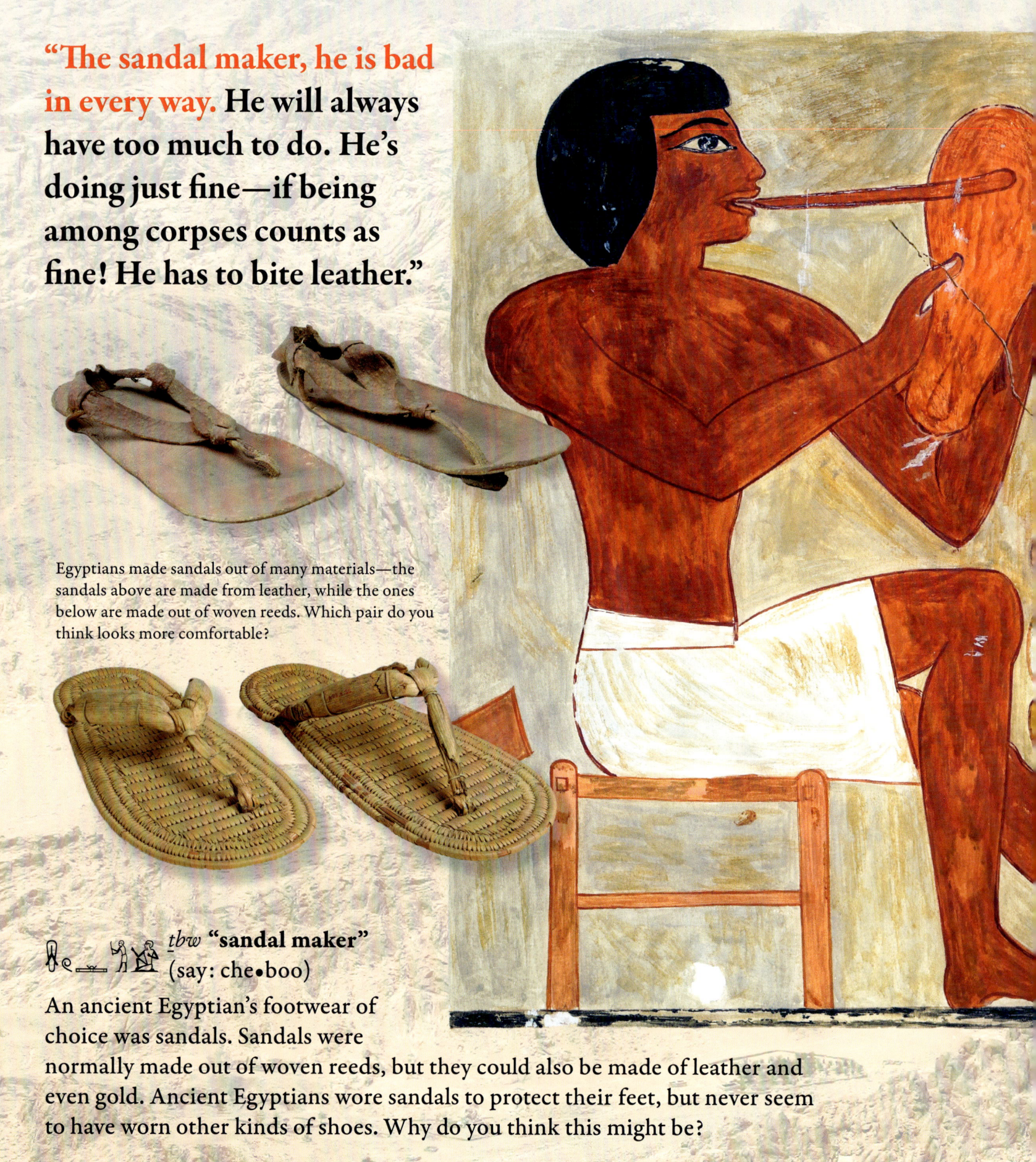

This sandal maker uses his teeth as an extra tool!

These golden sandals are too fragile for regular use. They were buried with a king's wife, but were probably not worn while she was alive.

## "He's doing just fine—if being among corpses counts as fine!"

Earlier, you read a similar phrase: "He's doing just fine—if being among lions counts as fine!" Both of these sayings are similar to the English "stuck in the mud" or "between a rock and a hard place." Every culture, and every language, has vivid phrases like these to describe tough situations. Cultures create sayings about things that are familiar to them, but these don't always translate well for people 4,000 years later. These corpses could also be the animal hides the sandal maker works with every day.

## "He has to bite leather."

Have you ever chewed on a leather belt or the ties of a baseball glove? Is the idea of having a piece of leather in your mouth really that unpleasant? Ancient Egyptian sandal makers had to do something like this all the time. In order to keep their hands free to work with their tools, they had to hold a piece of the sandal they were working on between their teeth. Here, Khety seems to be suggesting that biting leather is gross in order to make the sandal maker's job seem worse.

# The Launderer

"**The launderer launders on the riverbank,** with the crocodile as his neighbor. When he goes out on the water of the canal, his son and daughter say: "There is no job for you that is more peaceful, this job is easier than any other." But the kneading of clothes happens in his bathroom, and his body is never clean. He washes other people's clothing—even clothes with blood on them! He will cry spending a day with a washer's bat and a stone. He says: 'Please come to me, jar of cleaning solution. Don't overflow the rim!'"

Ancient Egyptian buckets were made of clay. This one might have been used to do laundry.

*rhty* **"launderer"** (say: rekh•tee)

Today, most of us use washing machines to do our laundry indoors. In ancient Egypt, it was a bit more complicated. For one thing, it had to be done by hand with a washer's bat and a stone, making it a tiring and repetitive process. Beyond that, it had to be done on a riverbank, out in the open (no indoor plumbing!). What's more, launderers weren't the only ones visiting the river: crocodiles lurked below the surface of the water, adding danger to an already difficult job.

This photo from the early 1900s shows Egyptian people washing clothes in the Nile.

This painting from more than 100 years ago shows launderers on the banks of the Nile. Not much had changed from ancient practices.

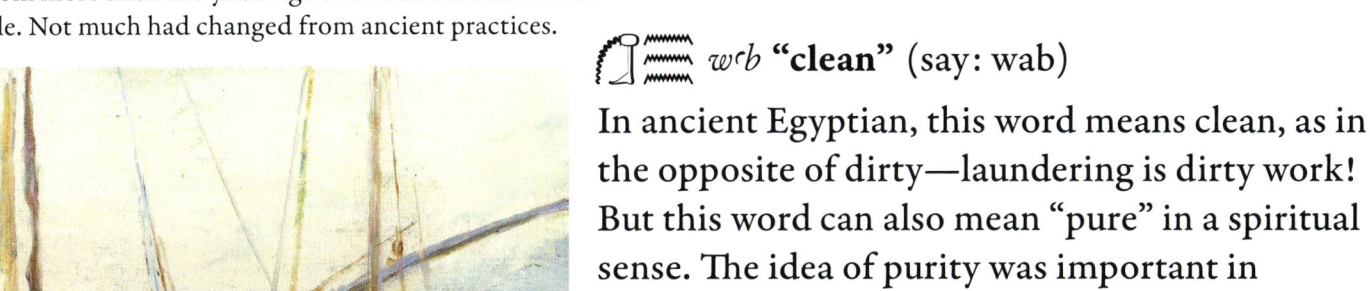

*wꜥb* **"clean"** (say: wab)

In ancient Egyptian, this word means clean, as in the opposite of dirty—laundering is dirty work! But this word can also mean "pure" in a spiritual sense. The idea of purity was important in Egyptian religion. In fact, in Egyptian temples, officials known as *wab* priests were responsible for keeping the temples clean and pure. Is Khety suggesting that the launderer is at the opposite end of this scale?

**"this job is easier than any other."**
The launderer's kids tell him this, and they seem to think his job is great. But a lot of jobs look fun until you actually have to start doing them! In fact, this whole story is about how adults and children perceive the world differently. The water of the canal might look peaceful, but there are crocodiles lurking underneath.

# The Bird Catcher

"**The bird catcher, he is miserable in every way** when he sees birds. If a flock passes over him, he will say, 'Oh, if only I had nets!' But no god wills it to happen. They are ignoring his plan."

*wh'w* **"bird catcher"** (say: we•ha•oo)

While wealthy ancient Egyptians could afford to eat beef and lamb, other people got their protein from fish and birds. In order to trap ducks and other birds to eat, bird catchers would use clapnets. They would lie in wait beside their clapnet, ready to pull a string that would shut the two halves and trap the birds inside.

The woman in this sculpture is carrying a basket of food on her head and a bird in her right hand. Her dress is made of feathers.

This man is hunting for birds with a clapnet—there is probably some kind of bait inside to lure the birds to their doom.

58

*iry pt* **"bird"** (say: ee•ree pet)

This phrase, translated here as "bird," literally means something like "sky fellow." There are many different words for bird in the Egyptian language, and Khety chose an especially poetic one here. Ancient Egyptian art and writing is almost as full of birds as Egypt itself—more than 200 species are known from ancient Egypt, and about 100 of them can be identified from their art, artifacts, and hieroglyphic signs alone! Egyptian artists observed nature closely, and birds perhaps most of all. We can still identify the precise species of birds from ancient paintings. It's safe to say that ancient Egyptians loved birds, so it's no surprise that they would invent fun names for them.

Throwsticks like this one were used to hunt birds. They were like ancient Egyptian boomerangs.

This man returns from the hunt with a large catch.

In ancient Egypt, hunting birds was both a way to earn a living and a popular sport. This scene from the tomb of a man named Menna shows a family on a day of leisure hunting and fishing in the papyrus marshes.

Hunting birds with a throwstick

Fishing with a spear

# The Fisherman

**"I will speak to you about how it is to be a fisherman:** he is more miserable than a person with any other job. There are no wages from the river—except the ones shared with crocodiles. If the crocodile doesn't get his fair share, he will make a complaint. He doesn't say 'there's a crocodile!' because fear has blinded him. When he goes out onto the water of the canal, the crocodile seems like the wrath of a god. Look, there is no profession without a boss—except for the scribe, he is the boss."

This man cuts the fish to clean it.

*wḥꜥw rmw* **"fisherman"**
(say: weh•hah•oo rem•oo)

Ancient Egyptian fishermen used tools similar to the ones we use today: harpoons, nets, and fishing lines with hooks attached (much like modern fishing rods). Just like birds in the previous section, fish were a common and cheap source of protein for ordinary people, who could rarely afford more luxurious meats such as beef. They also prepared the fish in similar manners to modern chefs: pickling, roasting, or drying. While fishing may have been a fun activity, even a pastime for many people, it was also dangerous business.

This tomb scene shows fishmongers at work.

> "Look, there is no profession without a boss—except for the scribe, he is the boss."

Who do you think is the fisherman's boss in this section? What point do you think Khety is trying to get across by saying that even fishermen have bosses?

> "There are no wages from the river—except the ones shared with crocodiles"

Imagine having crocodiles as your co-workers! That was the reality for ancient Egyptian fishermen. While *Be a Scribe!* casts crocodiles in a playful light, they did, in fact, pose a serious threat to anyone who worked on the Nile in ancient Egypt, including fishermen.

This man empties his catch.

This blue crocodile amulet is made from a type of ceramic called faience.

> "the crocodile seems like the wrath of a god."

While Khety does not name a single god here, there is good reason to think that he is referring to Sobek. Sobek was the crocodile god of ancient Egypt. According to ancient Egyptian religious writings, every crocodile in the land was a child of Sobek, and at the same time, one of his representatives in the real world. When a crocodile ate a fisherman, he was acting on the behalf of Sobek, who may have been angry at the fisherman for one reason or another. Perhaps for eating too many of his fish!

This fish-shaped object was used to grind eye makeup.

61

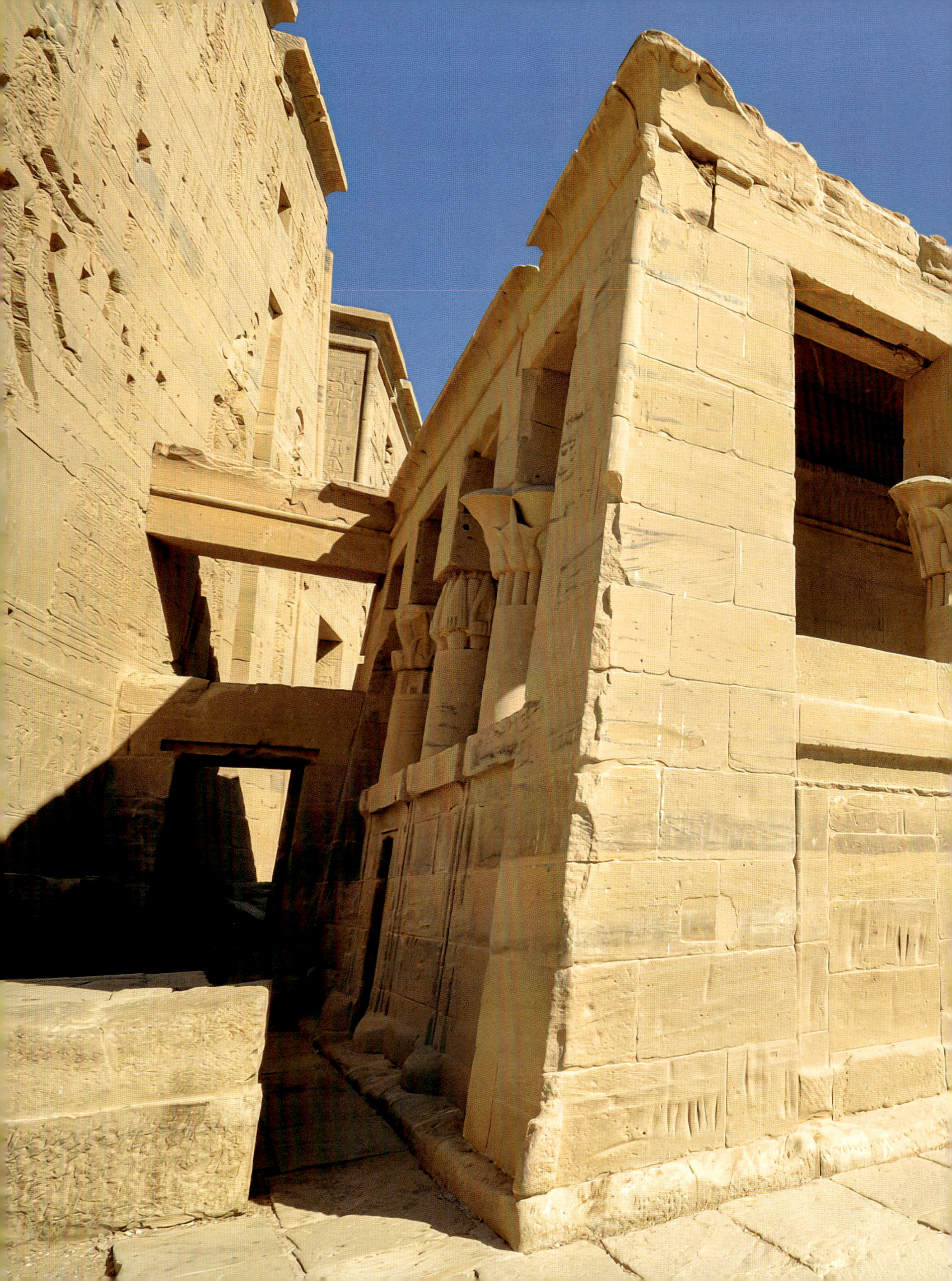

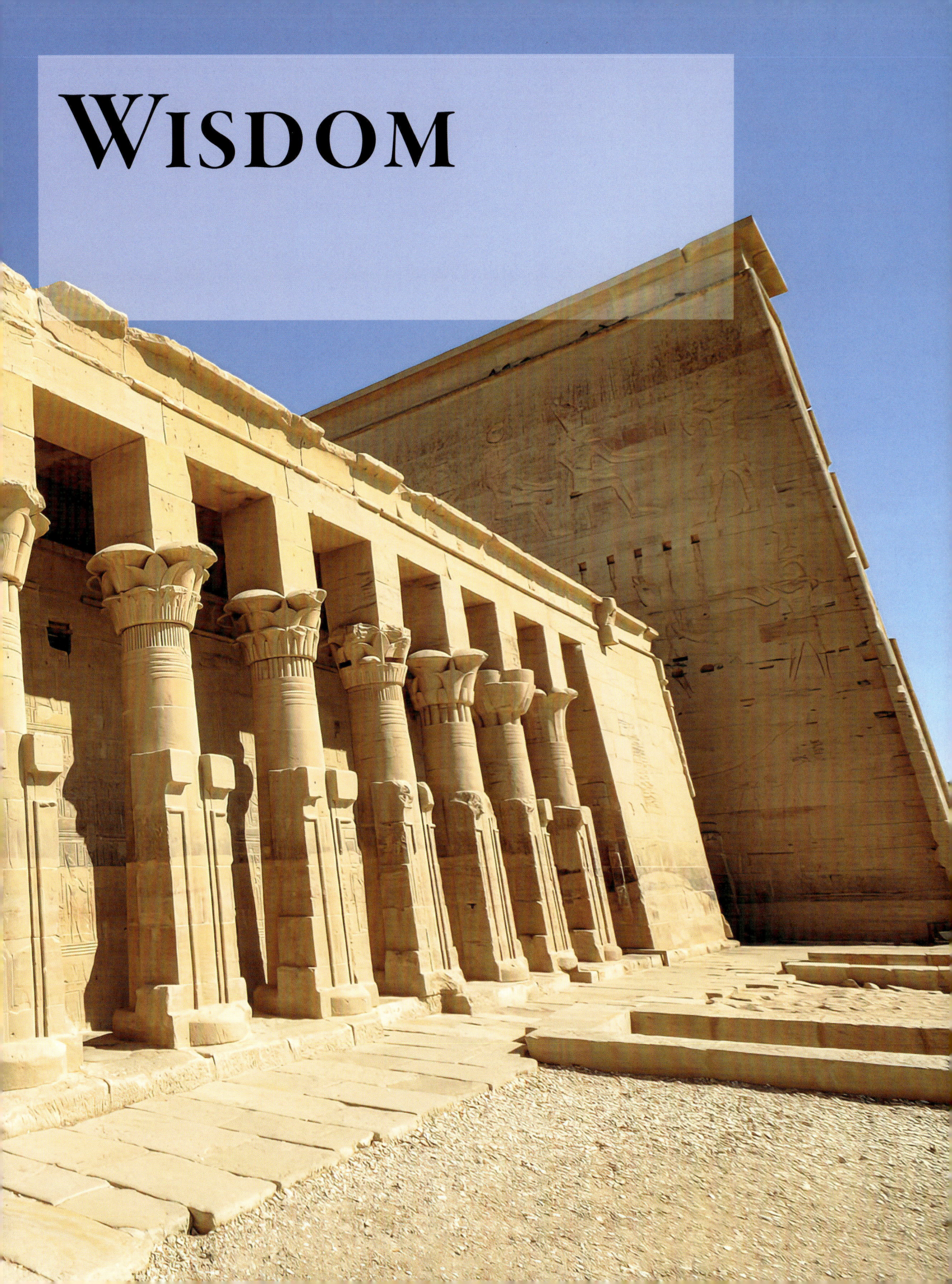

# Wisdom

# Be a Scribe!

**"But if you know how to write,** it will be good for you, better than the jobs I have shown you. The friend of a poor man may be a true friend, but a farmhand can't say to his boss: 'Don't boss me around!' This is why we are sailing upstream to the capital. I am doing it for your sake. A day in the classroom will do you good. Meanwhile, I will always be working in the mines. Hurry, hurry, I will teach you how to get rid of disobedience."

Seated scribe statues were often placed in temple courtyards as offerings to the gods.

This Egyptian necklace is made with turquoise mined in the Sinai desert. It's a symbol of Hathor, the goddess worshiped in those mines.

### ⦿ ‖ *zp 2* **"two times"** (say: zep 2)

In English writing, if a word is meant to be read twice, it's written twice. But in ancient Egyptian, things work differently: the word is written only once, followed by the phrase *zep 2*. Here Khety wants to say "hurry, hurry!", with the word doubled for special emphasis, but instead he writes, "hurry zep 2." This is just one of the many fascinating quirks of the ancient Egyptian writing system.

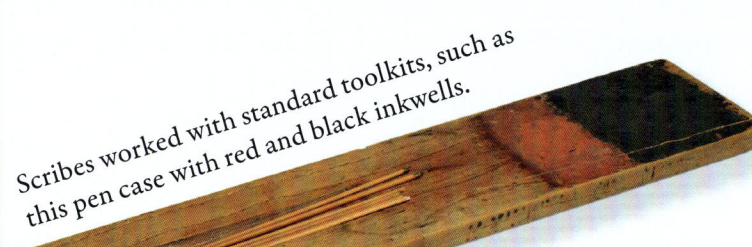

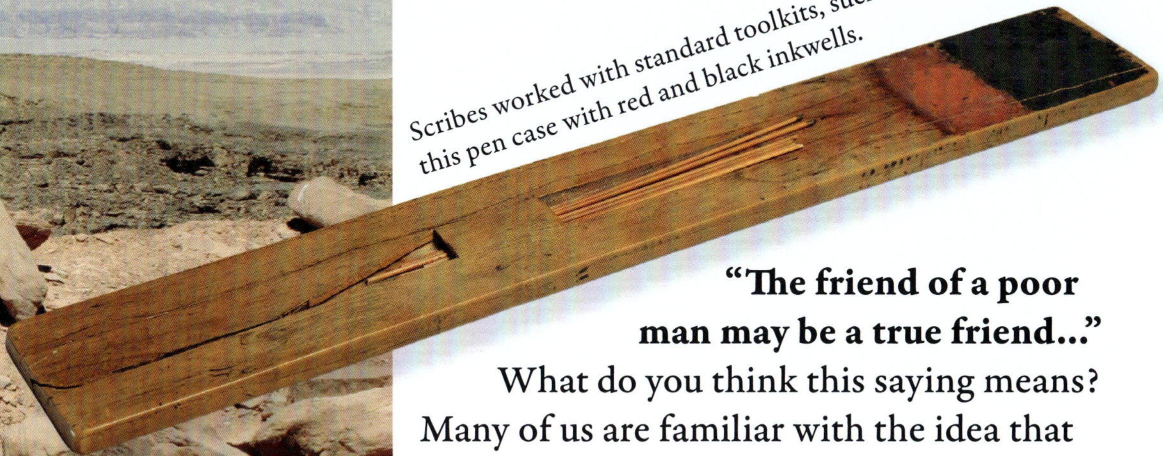

Scribes worked with standard toolkits, such as this pen case with red and black inkwells.

## "The friend of a poor man may be a true friend..."

What do you think this saying means? Many of us are familiar with the idea that "a friend in need is a friend indeed"—in other words, someone who remains friends with you even during a time of need is a true friend, rather than someone who only befriends you when you have something to offer them. The Egyptian saying is almost identical. It seems that this idea transcends place and time.

The first alphabetic writing appears on small carvings on stones found in the Sinai desert.

## "Meanwhile, I will always be working in the mines."

Remember that Khety lives in Sile, a city near the northeastern Nile Delta (see map on page 14). Sile was a major stopping point between the rest of Egypt and the important mines in the Sinai desert. Here Khety gives us a glimpse into his own background: he has something resembling a "blue-collar" job, but he wants his son to become a scribe and have an easier life than he has had himself.

## Miners in the Sinai invented the alphabet!

Did you know that the alphabet used to write English and many other modern languages comes from Egyptian hieroglyphs? It all started with miners from Canaan working in the Sinai alongside Egyptians like Khety. Canaanites could not read the Egyptian inscriptions they saw, but they could recognize the hieroglyphs, which represented everyday things. They gave names to hieroglyphic symbols in their own language. For instance, they identified the bull's head in ancient Egyptian with their own word for bull, *alp*. That symbol later became the *alpha* in Greek and the "a" in our alphabet. Notice how our capital letter A looks just like an upside-down bull's head.

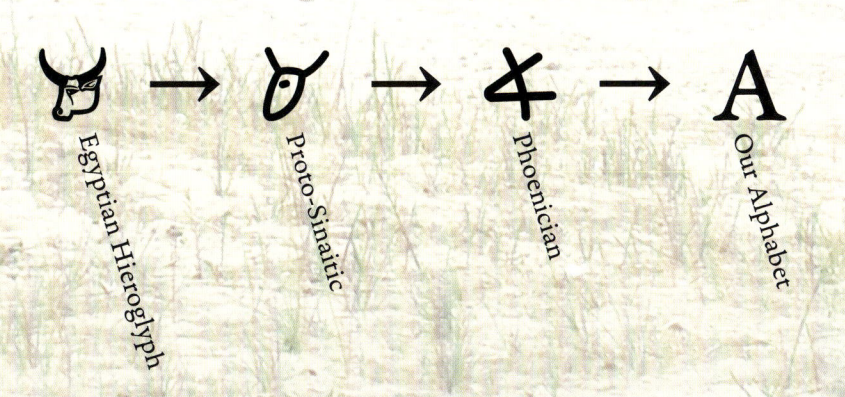

Egyptian Hieroglyph → Proto-Sinaitic → Phoenician → Our Alphabet

Our alphabet evolved from Egyptian hieroglyphs thanks to Canaanite miners working in the Sinai.

# STAY OUT OF TROUBLE...

**"I will tell you another idea:** in order to be educated you must learn. Stay away from fighting. You are among people who have bricks in their plans. If someone picks up a brick, run! You can't know what he is planning. When you testify before a judge, answer him thoughtfully and with deliberation."

*Elephant tusks were one source of ivory for ancient Egyptians.*

These hieroglyphs are some of the oldest ever discovered. They are written on ebony wood.

**What's the connection between someone with bricks in their plans and testifying in court?**
We aren't entirely sure why Khety chose to talk about these two things at the same time. However, it's interesting to note that both of these situations involve someone who has more power, and someone who has less.

Both a judge and a person holding a brick have control over someone's fate. Perhaps Khety wants his son to know that when he has less power, he should be careful about what he says and does.

Oases are isolated areas of water, trees, and life inside a vast unforgiving desert.

𓂧𓃀𓏏 *dbt* **"brick"** (say: de•bet)

Brick is one of the few ancient Egyptian words that survives in present-day English. It evolved into the word "adobe." Some other examples include "oasis," "ivory," "ebony," and "paper." Interestingly, even the word "gum" (as in chewing gum) comes from ancient Egyptian. It was originally a word for tree resin, which people chewed like modern gum.

Modern Egyptian chewing gum made with tree resin

Did you know that gum grows on trees?

An ancient Egyptian brick, inscribed with the cartouche of a king

This "ancient" chewing gum, called gum arabic, was tough and chewy like today's.

**"You are among people who have bricks in their plans."**

It's not exactly clear what this sentence means, but it might be Khety's way of warning his son about the dangers of the capital city. Maybe people with "bricks in their plans" are people who are scheming for political power and aren't afraid to use violence—throwing bricks—to achieve their goals. This might be the only surviving example of this Egyptian saying. What do you think?

67

# Mind Your Manners

**"If you walk behind officials,** don't be too near, it is far from good manners. If you enter when the lord is in his house, and he is talking to someone else, sit with your mouth shut and don't ask for anything. Do what he wants you to and don't join his table."

**What does an official do?**
Officials had some of the most important jobs in ancient Egypt— they managed the affairs of the country for the king! They oversaw agriculture, building projects, the collection of taxes, and more. As in the rest of Egyptian society, there was a hierarchy among officials. A very important official, whom Egyptologists call a vizier, was at the top, while local officials with more specific duties were further down. Even though most officials were born into their positions, some were not and had to work their way up.

**"don't join his table"**
To the ancient Egyptians, a table was a symbol of abundance and wealth. Many tomb scenes (such as the one to the right) show tables piled high with food and drink. To be invited to a powerful person's table was a great honor. But sitting at his table uninvited would be quite rude indeed.

This elegant chair belonged to a scribe named Reniseneb.

An official and his wife receive funerary offerings in the afterlife.

This low table is made of alabaster, a cream-colored stone with natural bands of white.

**"If you enter when the lord is in his house"**
The title "lord" was a sign that someone held a high position in society. What made someone a lord in ancient Egypt? He had to own land, rent it out to tenant farmers (see page 44), and collect a portion of the harvest from them as payment for the use of his land. In this way, lords in ancient Egypt were similar to small business owners today.

This 3,500-year-old wooden table looks like it could have been made today!

69

# Don't Blab!

**"Have the dignity of someone who is well respected. Don't speak about private matters. The more discreet you are, the better shielded you will be. Don't speak boastfully when the person sitting with you is being confrontational."**

A ceremonial shield from the tomb of Tutankhamun

This sculpture of a young official shows him wearing a stylish wig. Wigs were a status symbol in ancient Egypt and were often worn by officials (and men more generally).

**"The more discreet you are…"**
Literally, the original ancient Egyptian sentence reads, "the more you shield your belly…" How could shielding one's belly relate to being discreet? Ancient Egyptians thought that emotional thinking and "gut" instincts happened in the belly. Shielding your belly means concealing your true emotions in favor of being calm and rational. Unlike someone ruled by their emotions, a calm, rational person would be careful with what they say and do, and so be discreet.

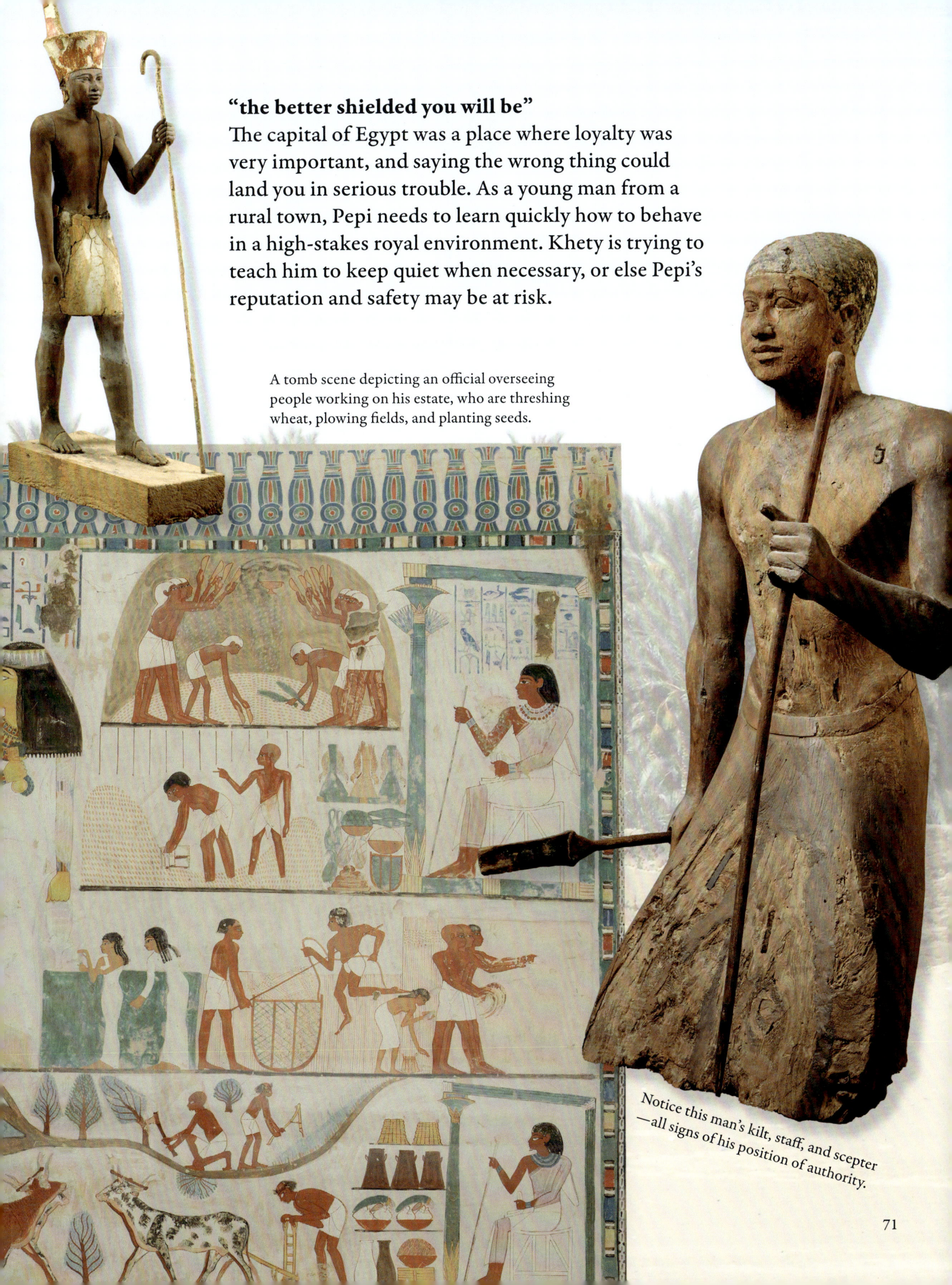

### "the better shielded you will be"

The capital of Egypt was a place where loyalty was very important, and saying the wrong thing could land you in serious trouble. As a young man from a rural town, Pepi needs to learn quickly how to behave in a high-stakes royal environment. Khety is trying to teach him to keep quiet when necessary, or else Pepi's reputation and safety may be at risk.

A tomb scene depicting an official overseeing people working on his estate, who are threshing wheat, plowing fields, and planting seeds.

Notice this man's kilt, staff, and scepter—all signs of his position of authority.

# Don't Play Hooky

"**If you leave school** at lunchtime and wander about in the streets, someone will punish you afterward, saying, 'you aren't supposed to do that.'"

**"someone will punish you..."**
How worried are you about getting in trouble at school? If you lived in ancient Egypt, you'd probably be a lot more worried. An ancient Egyptian saying goes, "A boy's ears are on his back; he hears when he is beaten." Some ancient Egyptians believed that children would listen only after they were physically punished. Remember what you read earlier—"I have seen many beatings" (page 20)—that physical punishment was much more common in ancient Egyptian society than in many modern ones. Even children couldn't escape it.

A wooden model of a scribe holding a long scribal palette with inkwells

This stone carving shows scribes at work.

*ꜥt-sbꜣ* **"school"**
(say: at•se•ba)

Very little is known about school buildings in ancient Egypt. Archaeologists haven't found any. However, they have found tomb scenes showing students sitting in class, listening carefully to their teacher and copying down his words on their writing boards. What would the teacher be reading aloud? Often wisdom texts like the one we are reading right now! In fact, many copies of *Be a Scribe!* were written down by students learning to write.

A wooden model of a kneeling scribe holding a papyrus scroll

A scribal student transcribed an Egyptian text onto this wooden writing board, and the teacher made corrections in red ink.

# Follow Orders

**"If an official sends you with a message,** say it like he says it. Don't leave anything out and don't add anything in. If you leave out even a *hin*, your name will not be trusted. When you gain mastery in all of your qualities, there will be nothing hidden from you and you can go anywhere."

### "say it like he says it"
In ancient Egypt, there were no phones. There wasn't even a fully developed postal service, though people did send letters. For the most part, people communicated using speech. Very important officials in the capital would send people to relay messages for them. A scribe tasked with such an errand would want to be very careful to get the message right!

This jar holds exactly one *hin*.

This ivory cylinder seal was used to roll the owner's name onto clay.

This scarab was inscribed with a person's name and designed to accompany their heart to the afterlife. In ancient Egypt, names were eternal.

*ḥn* **"hin"** (say: hen)

A *hin* is an amount of liquid (roughly equal to one pint or half a liter). For example, when Egyptians drank beer, they measured it in *hins*. When Khety says "hin" here, he means a small amount of something. It's like saying that someone doesn't have an ounce of sense.

Following orders is about respect, and not just among officials. This scene shows a mother and son sitting together in the afterlife. He must have respected his mother very much in life.

Most beer was drunk from simple clay jars. When this one was found, it had beer yeast inside.

This figure was mysteriously cut out of the scene!

This signet ring was used to stamp Tutankhamun's name onto documents.

*rn* **"name"** (say: ren)

Ancient Egyptians placed a lot of value on a person's name. It was one of the five essential parts of the person, beside the mind, shadow, *ba* (spirit), and *ka* (life force). Much more than a mere label, the name connected directly to who someone was at their core. Thus, to have a bad name would not just change how you were seen, it would change you for the worse.

# Control Yourself

"**Don't speak lies about anyone's mother**—officials don't want you to. If a man sells something of value and the deal is fair, then he has a good conscience. Don't egg on a confrontational person. He is already miserable. The belly of a man who listens to you belongs to you. If you are full with three pieces of bread and have swallowed two *hins* of beer, remember that bellies have no limit—fight against it! If another person is done and wants to stand up, don't remain seated."

**"The belly of a man who listens to you belongs to you"**
Ancient Egyptians believed that practical decisions were made with your heart, and emotional decisions were made with your belly. Maybe you, too, have been able to persuade someone to be on your side using emotion rather than reason. If a person listens to you with their belly, then they are more likely to be on your side.

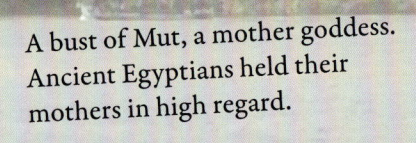

A bust of Mut, a mother goddess. Ancient Egyptians held their mothers in high regard.

**"If a man sells something of value and the deal is fair, then he has a good conscience"**
Literally, the original ancient Egyptian sentence says, "If he sells property and his two arms are alike, then his heart is merciful." This is probably a way of describing a fair deal. Just as the two arms of a scale are equal when both sides are in balance, a man's arms can be "alike" when he has made a fair deal.

Scales represented justice and fairness in ancient Egyptian society.

Pounding flour

Sifting the flour to make it finer

Bread was a major part of the Egyptian diet, but they ate other baked goods too. This collection of tomb paintings shows the process of making tiger nut cakes, a type of pastry.

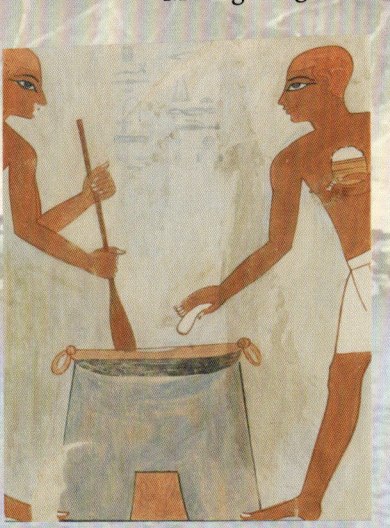

Mixing dough and adding a liquid to prepare it for the baking process

Adding fat

Baking the dough into cakes

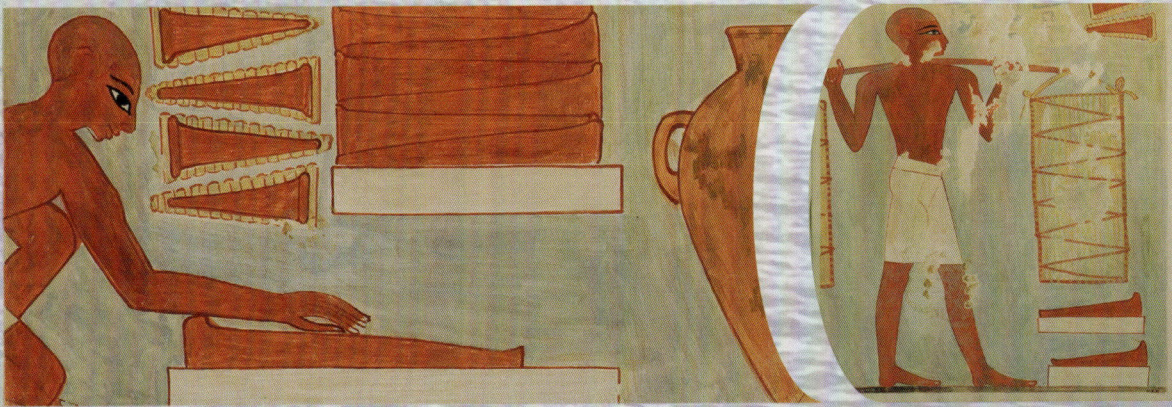

Taking the cakes out of the oven

Delivering the cakes

77

# Be Gumptious

**"Look, it's good that you send many letters home.** You should listen to what the officials say. Mimic the manners of the children of respectable people when you walk in their footsteps. You can always see a scribe being obedient, and obedient people become leaders. Fight words that are against initiative. You should hurry your legs when you are going. If you aren't trusted yet, associate with someone who is more distinguished than you, but also befriend a man of your generation."

This official is the kind of person the young Pepi would take orders from.

**What is gumption?** People who are gumptious are determined, confident, energetic, hardworking, and alert. In other words, they're just the opposite of lazy.

This scene shows children showing respect to their parents in the afterlife. They must have had good manners!

**"You should hurry your legs when you are going."**
Even though this line was pulled straight from an ancient Egyptian story that is almost 4,000 years old, it sounds remarkably similar to modern-day advice that warns against laziness. To the ancient Egyptians, legs were a symbol of work, motion, and productivity. The phrase "hurry your legs" might be a metaphor for working hard, but it could also be perfectly literal: "don't dilly-dally." What do you think?

To many of us, hands are a symbol of hard work. But to the ancient Egyptians, legs fulfilled that role: the hieroglyphic sign depicting a pair of legs appears in many words related to movement and action.

Ancient Egyptians sent letters both near and far! The letter on the left is written in cuneiform, another ancient writing system, and came to Egypt all the way from Tyre, in modern-day Lebanon. The letter below is an ancient Egyptian letter written in hieratic, just like the original version of this story.

# Fate Is Your Friend

"**Look, fate is controlled by the gods,** but the fate of a scribe is on his own shoulders from the day of his birth until he arrives at Areryt. This court has been made by people. Look, there is no scribe lacking food or any other thing from the palace (life, prosperity, and health). Meskhenet is a scribe's good fortune, he is placed at the front of the court. Thank your father and mother for putting you on the way of the living. Look at this which I have done for you and for the children of your children. This is how it comes to an end in peace."

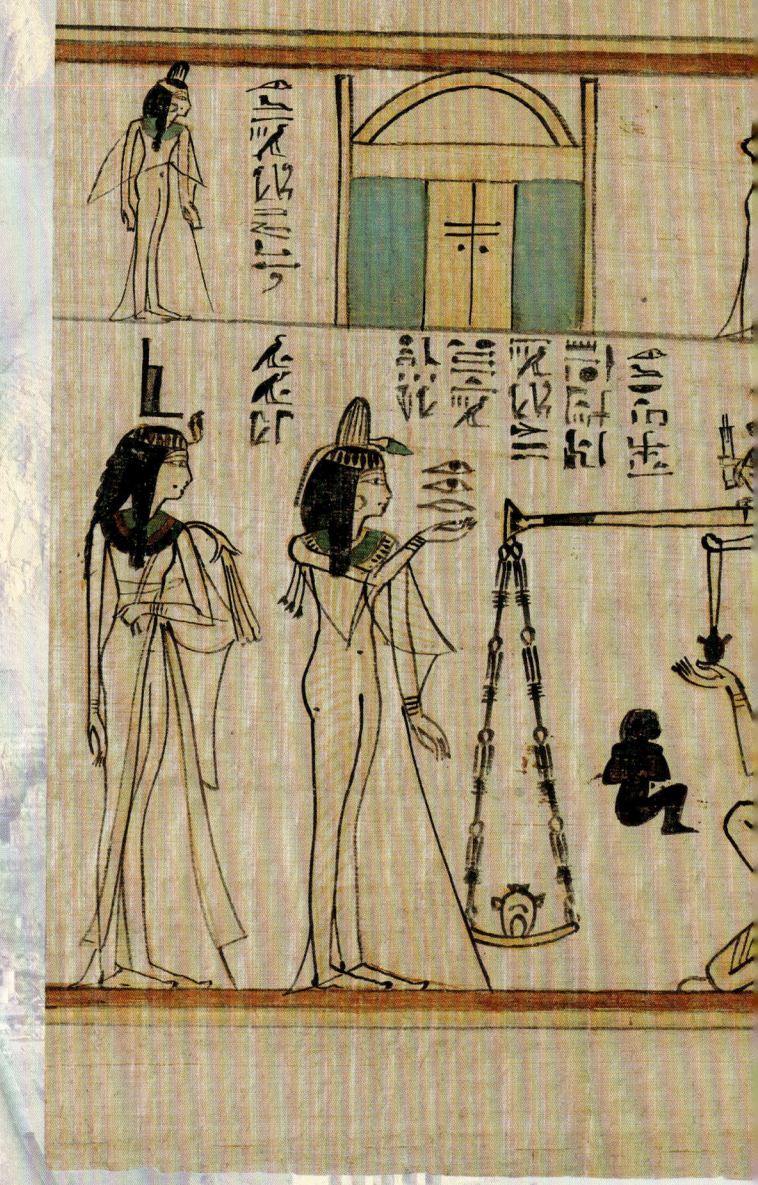

This wall carving depicts a goddess squatting over a birthing brick.

*mshnt* "**Meskhenet**" (say: mes•khe•net)
Ancient Egyptian women gave birth in a squatting position, on top of special "birthing" bricks. Every birthing brick was a representative of the goddess Meskhenet (just like every crocodile was a representative of Sobek, in the section on "The Fisherman" on page 60). In fact, Meskhenet is often depicted with a human head and a brick-shaped body. She had an important power: she determined the fate of every newborn child. By saying Meskhenet "is a scribe's good fortune," Khety means that scribes have the most blessed life from birth to death and beyond.

This papyrus from the Book of the Dead depicts *Areryt*, the court of judgment in the afterlife. Anubis, in the center, weighs the heart of the recently deceased against a feather to determine whether that person lived a moral life, while Osiris looks on.

ꜥrryt **"Areryt"** (say: ah•re•reet)

Literally, this word means the outer gate of a royal palace or court, where court cases would be held. Over time, this word began to shift in meaning from a physical gate to a court of law. Eventually, *Areryt* came to mean not just a court of law on earth, but a court of law where the souls of the dead would be judged by the gods.

ꜥnḫ wḏꜣ snb

**"life, prosperity, and health"**
(say: ankh we•dja se•neb)

This is an ancient Egyptian abbreviation, a lot like abbreviations in English such as NASA or NBA. doesn't translate well into English, but it means something like "life, prosperity, and health." Ancient Egyptians wrote it in letters when they wanted to send good wishes to each other. Here, it's used after "palace"—a word related to the king—to show respect for royal authority.

This stone carving depicts the goddess Meskhenet as a brick with a woman's face on it.

81

# Acknowledgments

This book would never have been possible without the generous and selfless support of many friends, colleagues, and family members. First, we would like to thank our wonderful team at Callaway: Nicholas Callaway for believing in this book, Manuela Roosevelt for all her wisdom and patient leadership through the difficult process of bringing the book to life, and Jason Brown, Toshiya Masuda, and True Sims for their expert help with the book's design. We are also indebted to Joel Tippie, who designed the book's cover, constructing a beautiful and historically accurate artwork from real ancient tomb scenes. Our proofreader, Janice Fisher, helped us improve the quality of the book by catching the errors that we failed to notice.

There are also people the authors would like to thank individually. Michael is forever grateful to his parents, brother, and family for their love and support throughout the whole book-writing process, and to Will Fitzhugh, the editor of the *Concord Review*, for sparking his interest in history. Michael would also like to thank Rick Richter for his support and guidance through the publishing process. Christian is grateful to at least two Egyptologists: Judith Jurjens, for her exciting work on an updated scholarly edition of *The Satire on the Trades* and her valuable insights into this difficult text, and James P. Allen, for too many things to mention, but especially for his help with challenging portions of the Egyptian manuscript. Jen is grateful for the personal and professional support of Jim and Susan Allen, James Grice, Claudia Glatz, Andreas Winkler, Carl Walsh, Vicky Almansa-Villatoro, Julia Troche, and Connie Gibilaro throughout this book project. She would also like to thank her colleagues at the Harvard Art Museums, Metropolitan Museum of Art, British Museum, Louvre Museum, National Archaeological Museum of Florence, and Institute for the Study of Ancient Cultures for the images that appear throughout this book.

## Learn More

Learn more about life in ancient Egypt, how to read hieroglyphs, and download Teachers' Guide material by visiting:

https://www.beascribe.com

# About the Images

All of the artifacts you've seen throughout this book are located in museums today. Here is a list of what you've seen in each section, including the object's title, the time when it was made, what materials it was made from, where it came from (if we know), how it got to the museum where it is today, and the object number that museum has given it. To find out more about an object, search for its object number on the website of the museum where it lives.

For the modern objects in this book, including paintings of ancient tomb scenes, you can search for more information on the websites listed here.

**The following abbreviations are used:**

*Met* = Metropolitan Museum of Art in New York (www.metmuseum.org). Courtesy of the Metropolitan Museum of Art. The authors are grateful to the Metropolitan Museum of Art for making images of their collection freely available to everyone.

*BM* = British Museum, London (www.britishmuseum.org). Courtesy of the British Museum.

*Harvard* = Harvard Art Museums in Cambridge, Massachusetts (www.harvardartmuseums.org/collections). Courtesy of the Harvard Art Museums.

*obj. no.* = object number

## Contents

Background image: **Egypt as seen from a satellite**. Photo by NASA/GSFC/Jeff Schmaltz/MODIS Land Rapid Response Team, uploaded by Wikipedia user A1Cafel.

## Introduction

Background image: **Giza pyramids**. Photo by Morhaf Kamal Aljanee.

**Sphinx of Amenhotep III** from 1390–1352 BCE. Made of faience (a type of ceramic). Purchased by the Met, obj. no. 1972.125.

**Gameboard** from 1550–1295 BCE. Made of faience (a type of ceramic) and reconstructed with modern wood. Excavated in a tomb at Abydos and then given to the Met, obj. no. 01.4.1.

**Gazelle figurine** from 1390–1352 BCE. Made of wood, ivory, and blue paint inlays. Purchased by the Met, obj. no. 26.7.1292.

**Festival scene**. Modern copy of an ancient painting in the tomb of a priest named Amenmose at Thebes from 1295–1213 BCE. Painted on paper at Thebes by artist Charles K. Wilkinson in the 1920s for the Met, obj. no. 32.6.1.

## Ready to Learn Some Ancient Egyptian?

Background image: **Hieroglyphs carved in stone**. Photo by Alejandro Quintanar.

**A page from Papyrus Sallier II, the only papyrus with a complete copy of the story translated here** from 1295–1186 BCE. Written in ink. Purchased by the BM, obj. no. 10182.3. Photo courtesy of the British Museum.

**Inlays in the shapes of hieroglyphs** from 664–610

83

BCE. Made of faience (a type of ceramic), these small hieroglyph pieces were probably embedded in a piece of wooden furniture. The wood decayed over time and left these pieces behind. Excavated at Thebes in the tomb of an official named Nespekashuty by a team of archaeologists from the Met, obj. no. 26.3.164.

**Inlay in the shape of the Horus of Gold** from the 4th century BCE. Made of faience (a type of ceramic), this artifact depicts the falcon god Horus standing on the hieroglyph for gold, a common element in kings' names. Purchased by the Met, obj. no. 26.7.996.

# Timeline

Background image: **King list, Temple of Seti I at Abydos**. Photo © Kyera Giannini.

**Narmer Palette (showing the king Menes uniting Egypt)** from about 3100 BCE. Made of schist (a type of stone). Excavated at Hierakonpolis and brought to the Egyptian Museum in Cairo (www.egymonuments.gov.eg/en/museums/egyptian-museum), obj. no. JE32169. Photo by Wikipedia user Heagy1 (photo background removed).

**Great Pyramid of Khufu** from about 2570 BCE. Built from limestone, mortar, and granite (a type of stone). Located at Giza. Photo by Emőke Dénes (photo background removed).

**Statue of the king Mentuhotep II** from 2051–2000 BCE. Made of painted sandstone. Excavated in the temple of Mentuhotep II at Deir el-Bahari in Thebes by a team of archaeologists from the Met, obj. no. 26.3.29.

**Scene from a Book of the Dead belonging to a singer and priestess named Nauny** from about 1050 BCE. Made of painted papyrus. Excavated at Thebes in the tomb of the queen Ahmose-Meritamun by a team of archaeologists from the Met, obj. no. 30.3.31.

**Sculpture of the head of the king Ahmose I** from 1550–1525 BCE. Made of limestone. Donated to the Met, obj. no. 2006.270.

**Sculpture of the head of the king Hatshepsut** from 1479–1458 BCE. Made of painted limestone. Excavated at Deir el-Bahari in Thebes by a team of archaeologists from the Met, obj. no. 31.3.164.

**A page from Papyrus Sallier II, the only papyrus with a complete copy of the story translated here** from 1295–1186 BCE. Written in ink. Purchased by the BM, obj. no. 10182.3. Photo courtesy of the British Museum.

**Ostracon** from 1295–1070 BCE. Made of limestone with writing in ink. Excavated in the Valley of the Kings at Thebes and later donated to the Met, obj. no. 14.6.219.

**Sculpture of the head of Alexander the Great** from 300–150 BCE. Made of marble. Purchased by the BM, obj. no. 1872,0515.1. Photo by Wikipedia user Yair-haklai (photo background removed).

**Naval battle at Actium** from the 1st century CE. Made of marble. Located in the collection of the Dukes of Cardona in Cordoba, Spain. Photo by Mark Landon, uploaded by Wikipedia user Choliamb (photo background removed).

**Sculpture of the head of Cleopatra** from 40–30 BCE. Made of marble. Located at the Altes Museum in Berlin (https://www.smb.museum/en/museums-institutions/altes-museum/home), obj. no. 1976.10. Photo by Richard Mortel, uploaded by Wikipedia user Meisam (photo background removed).

**The last hieroglyphs** from August 24, 394 CE. Carved in sandstone. Located at Philae Temple. Photo by Olaf Tausch (photo background removed).

**Philae Temple** from the 7th century BCE–6th century CE. Built from stone. Located at the First Cataract of the Nile. Photo by Warren LeMay, uploaded by Wikipedia user Ser Amantio di Nicolao (photo cropped).

**Mosque of Amr ibn al-As**, originally from 642 CE. Located in Cairo. Photo by Mohammed Moussa (photo background removed).

**Book of prayers written in Coptic and Arabic** from the 17th–18th century CE. Made of paper with writing in ink. Excavated in Egypt by a team of archaeologists from the Met, obj. no. 19.196.3.

**Mosque lamp** from slightly later than 1285 CE. Made of glass and gold. Donated to the Met, obj. no. 17.190.985.

**Declaration of Independence**, original from 1776, this image reprinted by William Stone in 1823. Photo by Wikipedia user Parhamr.

# Journey

Artwork: **Medinet Habu, mortuary temple of Ramesses III** from 1847 by Louis Haghe, after David Roberts.

## On the River

Background image: **West bank of the Nile River at Luxor**. Photo © Vyacheslav Argenberg / www.vascoplanet.com.

**Model of a boat with rowers** from 1981–1975 BCE. Made of painted wood, plaster, linen twine, and linen fabric. Excavated at Thebes in the tomb of an official named Meketre by a team of archaeologists from the Met, obj. no. 20.3.1.

**Jar decorated with boats and human figures** from 3500–3300 BCE. Made of painted pottery. Purchased from Howard Carter by the Met, obj. no. 20.2.10.

**Statue of an official named Wah** from 1981–1975 BCE. Made of painted wood, plaster, and linen fabric. Excavated at Thebes in the tomb of Wah by a team of archaeologists from the Met, obj. no. 20.3.210.

## Fatherly Advice

Background image: **Lake Nasser, Egypt**. Photo by Dennis Jarvis.

**Scene of man being beaten** from 1400–1352 BCE. Made of paint and plaster. Located in the tomb of an official named Menna at Thebes. This image is from a 3D model of the tomb made by Tessa Litecky of the American Research Center in Egypt (www.arce.org). The full virtual tour is available here: https://my.matterport.com/show/?m=vLYoS66CWpk.

**Heart scarab belonging to a woman named Hatnefer** from 1492–1473 BCE. Made of serpentinite (a type of stone) and gold. Excavated at Thebes in the tomb of Hatnefer and Ramose by a team of archaeologists from the Met, obj. no. 36.3.2.

**Heart amulet** from 664–334 BCE. Made of lapis lazuli (a type of stone). Purchased by the Met, obj. no. 74.51.4445.

**Ostracon with writing similar to Kemyt** from 1295–1070 BCE. Made of pottery with writing in ink. From Karnak in Thebes, now at the BM, obj. no. EA21284. Photo courtesy of the British Museum.

## The Best Job

Background image: **Irrigated fields, Nile Delta, Egypt**. Photo by François Molle/IRD.

**Bird's eye view of a garden**. Modern copy of an ancient painting in the tomb of an official named Sennefer at Thebes from 1439–1413 BCE. Printed on paper. Photo by Wikipedia user Gmihail.

**Model of a granary with scribes** from 1981–1975 BCE. Made of painted wood, plaster, linen fabric, and real grain. Excavated at Thebes in the tomb of an official named Meketre by a team of archaeologists from the Met, obj. no. 20.3.11.

**Carving of ripe barley** from 1353–1336 BCE. Made of painted limestone. Donated to the Met, obj. no. 1985.328.24.

**Statue of a scribe named Merer with writing on his kilt** from 1981–1802 BCE. Made of painted wood and plaster. Purchased by the Met, obj. no. 10.176.59.

# Jobs

Photo: **Medinet Habu, mortuary temple of Ramesses III** © Vyacheslav Argenberg / www.vascoplanet.com.

## The Smith

Background image: **Quarry of the unfinished obelisk, Aswan**. Photo by Diego Delso, delso.photo, License CC-BY-SA.

**Sculptors at work**. Modern copy of an ancient painting in the tomb of an official named Rekhmire at Thebes from 1504–1425 BCE. Painted on paper at Thebes by artist Nina de Garis Davies in 1927 for the Met, obj. no. 30.4.90.

**Ring belonging to the priest Sienamun** from 664–525 BCE. Made of gold. Donated to the Met, obj. no. 23.10.14.

**A man at a forge**. Modern copy of an ancient painting in the tomb of an official named Rekhmire at Thebes from 1504–1425 BCE. Painted on paper at Thebes by artist Nina de Garis Davies in 1928 for the Met, obj. no. 31.6.22.

**Men pouring metal into a mold**. Modern copy of an ancient painting in the tomb of an official named Rekhmire at Thebes from 1504–1425 BCE. Painted on paper at Thebes by artist Nina de Garis Davies in 1927 for the Met, obj. no. 33.8.5.

**Statue of a cat** from 664–332 BCE. Made of bronze. Donated by Marian H. Phinney to Harvard, obj. no.1962.69. Photo © President and Fellows of Harvard College.

**Fish pendant** from 1981–1650 BCE. Made of gold and bronze. Donated to the Met, obj. no. 1971.272.2.

**Crucible with pieces of malachite (a copper ore)** from 1479–1458 BCE. Made of pottery. Excavated in the temple of Hatshepsut at Deir el-Bahari in Thebes by a team of archaeologists from the Met, obj. no. 25.3.95.

# The Carpenter

Background image: **Acacia tree in Ein Khadra Desert Oasis, Sinai**. Photo by لا روسا.

**A man trimming wood with an adze**. Modern copy of an ancient painting in the tomb of an official named Rekhmire at Thebes from 1504–1425 BCE. Painted on paper at Thebes by artist Nina de Garis Davies in 1928 for the Met, obj. no. 31.6.28.

**Carpenters at work**. Modern copy of an ancient painting in the tomb of an official named Rekhmire at Thebes from 1504–1425 BCE. Painted on paper at Thebes by artist Nina de Garis Davies in 1935 for the Met, obj. no. 35.101.1.

**Lamp** from 1981–1640 BCE. Made of pottery. Excavated in the cemetery at Lisht by a team of archaeologists from the Met, obj. no. 15.3.1391.

**Adze** from 1550–1295 BCE. Made of wood, bronze, and leather. Excavated in the temple of Hatshepsut at Deir el-Bahari in Thebes by a team of archaeologists from the Met, obj. no. 25.3.114.

# The Jeweler

Background image: **Summit of Mount Sinai**. Photo by Mohammed Moussa.

**Statue of the god Amun** from 945–712 BCE. Made of gold. Purchased by the Met, obj. no. 26.7.1412.

**People from Crete bringing gifts of metal and jewelry**. Modern copy of an ancient painting in the tomb of an official named Rekhmire at Thebes from 1504–1425 BCE. Painted on paper at Thebes by artist Nina de Garis Davies in 1926 for the Met, obj. no. 31.6.45.

**Jewelry elements** from 1878–1805 BCE. Made of gold and stones called carnelian and lapis lazuli. Purchased by the Met, obj. no. 26.7.1309–.1312.

**Jewelry box belonging to a woman named Rennefer** from 1504–1447 BCE. Made of faience (a type of ceramic) and reconstructed with modern wood. Excavated at Thebes in the tomb of Neferkhawet and Rennefer by a team of archaeologists from the Met, obj. no. 35.3.79.

**Ring with birds** from 1295–1185 BCE. Made of faience (a type of ceramic). Purchased by the Met, obj. no. 26.7.824.

**Necklace belonging to the princess Sithathoryunet with the name of the king Senwosret II** from 1887–1878 BCE. Made of gold and stones called carnelian, lapis lazuli, turquoise, garnet, and green feldspar. Excavated at Lahun in the tomb of a princess named Sithathoryunet and later purchased by the Met, obj. no. 16.1.3.

**Cuff bracelet** from 1479–1425 BCE. Made of gold, glass, and carnelian (a type of stone). Probably from the tomb of three wives of the king Tuthmosis III in Thebes. Purchased by the Met, obj. no. 26.8.129.

**Signet ring** from 1353–1323 BCE. Made of gold. Purchased by the Met, obj. no. 24.2.8.

**Men stringing and drilling beads**. Modern copy of an ancient painting in the tomb of an official named Rekhmire at Thebes from 1504–1425 BCE. Painted on paper at Thebes by artist Nina de Garis Davies in 1929 for the Met, obj. no. 31.6.25.

# The Barber

Background image: **The White Desert at night**. Photo by Ahmed Yousry Mahfouz.

**Cosmetic set with a tube for eye paint, razor, tweezers, whetstone, and mirror** from 1550–1458 BCE. Made of bronze, stone, ivory, and wood. Excavated in a burial at Thebes and later purchased by the Met, obj. no. 26.7.837.

**Razor belonging to a woman named Hatnefer** from 1492–1473 BCE. Made of bronze and wood. Excavated at Thebes in the tomb of Hatnefer and Ramose by a team of archaeologists from the Met, obj. no. 36.3.69.

**Funerary mask of Hatnefer** from 1492–1473 BCE. Made of cartonnage (linen strips and/or papyrus mixed with plaster), obsidian (a type of volcanic glass), travertine (a type of stone, also called Egyptian alabaster), ebony wood, and gold. Excavated at Thebes in the tomb of Hatnefer and Ramose by a team of archaeologists from the Met, obj. no. 36.3.1.

**Figurine of the god Horus as a child with a lock of hair on the side of his head** from late 8th–late 6th century BCE. Made of bronze. Donated by Elizabeth Gaskell Norton and Margaret Norton to Harvard, obj. no. 1920.44.303. Photo © President and Fellows of Harvard College.

**A barber working while customers wait in line**. Modern copy of an ancient painting in the tomb of a royal scribe named Userhat at Thebes from 1427–1400 BCE. Painted on paper at Thebes by artist Nina de Garis Davies in 1922 for the Met, obj. no. 30.4.40.

**Statue of a priest** from 589–570 BCE. Made of granodiorite (a type of stone). Donated to the Walters Art Museum in Baltimore, Maryland (www.thewalters.org), obj. no. 22.113.

# The Trader

Background image: **Papyrus sedge**. Photo by Wikipedia user pjt56.

**A papyrus marsh**. Modern copy of an ancient painting in the tomb of an official named Qenamun at Thebes from 1427–1400 BCE. Painted on paper at Thebes by artist Hugh R. Hopgood in 1914–1915 for the Met, obj. no. 30.4.60.

**A boat journeying to Abydos**. Modern copy of an ancient painting in the tomb of a priest named Pairy at Thebes from 1390–1352 BCE. Painted on paper at Thebes by artist Charles K. Wilkinson in 1926 for the Met, obj. no. 30.4.96.

**Model of a boat with rowers** from 1981–1975 BCE. Made of painted wood, plaster, linen twine, and linen fabric. Excavated at Thebes in the tomb of an official named Meketre by a team of archaeologists from the Met, obj. no. 20.3.2.

**Mosquito amulet** from 712–332 BCE. Made of jasper (a type of stone). Donated to the Met, obj. no. 55.172.

# The Potter

Background image: **Newly excavated drain, Nile Delta, Egypt**. Photo by François Molle/IRD.

**Model of a house** from 1750–1700 BCE. Made of pottery. Excavated in the cemetery of the ancient town of Shashotep and then given to the Met, obj. no. 07.231.11.

**Ushabti (funerary figurine) belonging to an official named Hekaemsaf** from 570–526 BCE. Made of faience (a type of ceramic). Excavated at Saqqara in the tomb of Hekaemsaf and later donated to the Met, obj. no. 2021.41.150.

**Man using a potter's wheel** from 2474–2444 BCE. Made of pottery. Purchased by the Institute for the Study of Ancient Cultures (formerly the Oriental Institute) in Chicago (www.isac-idb.uchicago.edu), obj. no. E10628. Courtesy of the Institute for the Study of Ancient Cultures of the University of Chicago.

**Brick makers using pots to collect water**. Modern copy of an ancient painting in the tomb of an official named Rekhmire at Thebes from 1504–1425 BCE. Painted on paper at Thebes by artist Nina de Garis Davies in 1925 for the Met, obj. no. 30.4.89.

**Vessel with handles and a lid** from 1353–1336 BCE. Made of pottery. Excavated in a house at Amarna and later donated to the Met, obj. no. 29.7.2.

**Bowl with human feet** from 3700–3450 BCE. Made of pottery. Purchased by the Met, obj. no. 10.176.113.

**Water bottle** from 1336–1327 BCE. Made of painted pottery. Excavated at Thebes in a group of objects from the funeral of the king Tutankhamun and later given to the Met, obj. no. 09.184.83.

# The Wall Builder

Background image: **Sandstorm seen from above**. Photo by Olga Ernst and Hp.Baumeler.

**Men making bricks**. Modern copy of an ancient painting in the tomb of an official named Rekhmire at Thebes from 1504–1425 BCE. Painted on paper at Thebes by artist Nina de Garis Davies in 1928 for the Met, obj. no. 30.4.77.

**Brick mold** from 1550–1295 BCE. Made of wood. Excavated in the temple of Hatshepsut at Deir el-Bahari in Thebes by a team of archaeologists from the Met, obj. no. 25.3.108.

**Model of a house** from 1550 BCE–395 CE. Made of limestone. Purchased by the Louvre Museum in Paris (https://www.louvre.fr/en), obj. no. E5357. Photo by Gary Todd, uploaded by Wikipedia user Tm (photo background removed).

**Brick with a stamp of an official named Senimen** from 1479–1458 BCE. Made of mudbrick. Excavated at Thebes by a team of archaeologists from the Met, obj. no. 14.1.425.

# The Roofer

Background image: **Village of Bashendi, Dakhla Oasis, Egypt**. Photo © NYU Excavations at Amheida / Institute for the Study of the Ancient World.

**Modern reconstruction of an ancient Egyptian house** from 2023. Taken from the video game Assassin's Creed Origins.

**Model of a house** from 1750–1700 BCE. Made of pottery. Excavated in the cemetery of the ancient town of Shashotep and then given to the Met, obj. no. 07.231.10.

**Cubit measuring rod** from 1981–1640 BCE. Made of wood. Excavated in the cemetery at Lisht by a team of archaeologists from the Met, obj. no. 15.3.1128.

**Piece of a measuring rod with fractions of a cubit** from 1550–1295 BCE. Made of slate. Purchased by the Met, obj. no. 25.7.41.

# The Gardener

Background image: **Aswan Botanical Garden**. Photo by Olaf Tausch.

**Men harvesting and stomping grapes**. Modern copy of an ancient painting in the tomb of a scribe named Nakht at Thebes from 1410–1370 BCE. Painted on paper at Thebes by a team of artists from 1908 to 1914 for the Met, obj. no. 15.5.19.

**Model of a porch and garden** from 1981–1975 BCE. Made of painted wood and copper. Excavated at Thebes in the tomb of an official named Meketre by a team of archaeologists from the Met, obj. no. 20.3.13.

**Gardener lifting water to his plants**. Modern copy of an ancient painting in the tomb of a sculptor named Ipuy at Thebes from 1295–1213 BCE. Painted on paper at Thebes by artist Norman de Garis Davies in 1924 for the Met, obj. no. 30.4.115.

**Model of a shoulder-yoke** from 1390–1352 BCE. Made of wood and bronze. Excavated at Thebes in the tomb of Yuya and Thuya (the parents of the queen Tiye) and later donated to the Met, obj. no. 30.8.63.

# The Tenant Farmer

Background image: **Wheat harvesting at an Egyptian village**. Photo by Amr Hamed.

**Model of a man plowing** from 1981–1885 BCE. Made of painted wood. Donated to the Met, obj. no. 36.5.

**Harvest scene with tax collectors**. Modern copy of an ancient painting in the tomb of an official named Menna at Thebes from 1400–1352 BCE. Painted on paper at Thebes by artist Charles K. Wilkinson in the 1920s for the Met, obj. no. 30.4.44.

**Sennedjem and his wife Iineferti farming in the afterlife**. Modern copy of an ancient painting in the tomb of an official named Sennedjem at Thebes from 1295–1213 BCE. Painted on paper at Thebes by artist Charles K. Wilkinson in 1922 for the Met, obj. no. 30.4.2.

# The Weaver

Background image: **Field of flax**. Photo by Nick O'Doherty.

**Weavers' shuttles** from 1295–1070 BCE. Made of wood. Excavated in the cemetery at Saqqara and then purchased by the Met, obj. nos. 26.2.37 and 26.2.36.

**Model of a weaving room** from 1981–1975 BCE. Made of painted wood, plaster, linen twine, and linen fabric. Excavated at Thebes in the tomb of an official named Meketre and brought to the Egyptian Museum in Cairo (www.egymonuments.gov.eg/en/museums/egyptian-museum), obj. no. JE46723.

**Fabric** from 818–700 BCE. Made of linen. Excavated in Fayum and then given to the Met, obj. no. 14.4.97.

**Weavers working**. Modern copy of an ancient painting in the tomb of an official named Khnumhotep at Beni Hasan from 1897–1878 BCE. Painted on paper at Beni Hasan by artist Norman de Garis Davies in 1931 for the Met, obj. no. 30.4.115.

# The Weapon Maker

Background image: **Desert landscape with palm trees**.

**Bow** from 1492–1458 BCE. Made of wood. Excavated at Thebes in the tomb of an official named Senenmut by a team of archaeologists from the Met, obj. no. 36.3.211.

**Donkeys with sacks of grain on their backs**. Modern copy of an ancient painting in the tomb of an official named Djar at Thebes from 2060–2010 BCE. Painted on paper at Thebes by artist Nina de Garis Davies in 1931 for the Met, obj. no. 31.6.2.

**Model of a shield, spear case, and spears** from 1981–1802 BCE. Made of painted wood and plaster. Purchased by the Met, obj. no. 17.9.3–.11.

**Battle axe belonging to a man named Baki** from 1504–1447 BCE. Made of bronze and wood and reconstructed with modern wood and animal skin. Excavated at Thebes in the tomb of Baki and his family by a team of archaeologists from the Met, obj. no. 35.3.56.

**Arrows with stone tips** from 1981–1550 BCE. Made of wood, flint (a type of stone), resin, and feathers. Purchased by the Met, obj. no. 12.182.53.

**Sword** from 1550–1458 BCE. Made of bronze. Excavated in a burial at Thebes by a team of archaeologists from the Met, obj. no. 16.10.453.

**Javelin** from 1492–1458 BCE. Made of wood, ivory, bark, and bronze. Excavated at Thebes in the tomb of an official named Senenmut by a team of archaeologists from the Met, obj. no. 36.3.206.

# The Courier

Background image: **Lebanese cedar trees**. Photo by Zeynel Cebeci.

**Sculptor's model of a lion** from 380–343 BCE. Made of limestone. Purchased by Harvard using the David M. Robinson Fund, obj. no. 1979.398. Photo © President and Fellows of Harvard College.

**Letter sent to a man named Merisu to ask him to rent some land for a man named Heqanakht** from 1961–1917 BCE. Made of papyrus with writing in ink. Excavated at Thebes in the tomb of an official named Ipy by a team of archaeologists from the Met, obj. no. 22.3.516.

**Leaders of the *Aamu***. Modern copy of an ancient painting in the tomb of an official named Khnumhotep at Beni Hasan from 1897–1878 BCE. Painted on paper at Beni Hasan by artist Norman de Garis Davies in 1931 for the Met, obj. no. 33.8.17.

**A tent in the Arabian desert**. Photo by Flickr user twiga-swala (photo background removed).

## The Leather Worker

Background image: **Water buffalo along the Nile River**. Photo by David Berkowitz (www.marketersstudio.com), uploaded by Wikipedia user Orizan.

**"Leopard-skin" robe belonging to a priest named Harnedjitef** from the 1st century CE. Made of painted linen. Purchased by the Met, obj. no. 31.9.4.

**Statue of a woman in a long dress** from 1981–1640 BCE. Made of painted wood. Excavated in the cemetery at Lisht by a team of archaeologists from the Met, obj. no. 11.151.745.

**Archer's wrist guard** from 1961–1917 BCE. Made of leather. Excavated at Thebes in the tomb of a group of soldiers by a team of archaeologists from the Met, obj. no. 27.3.135.

**Wood and leather craftsmen at work**. Modern copy of an ancient painting in the tomb of an official named Hapu at Thebes from 1400–1390 BCE. Painted on paper at Thebes by artist Nina de Garis Davies in 1927 for the Met, obj. no. 30.4.150.

## The Sandal Maker

Background image: **Mount Catherine on the Sinai Peninsula**. Photo by Gerd Eichmann.

**Leather sandals belonging to a child named Amenhotep** from 1479–1458 BCE. Made of red-stained cow's leather. Excavated at Thebes in the tomb of an official named Senenmut by a team of archaeologists from the Met, obj. no. 36.3.159.

**Reed sandals** from 1580–1479 BCE. Made of papyrus reeds. Excavated in a tomb at Thebes by the Met, obj. no. 22.3.20.

**Man making sandals**. Modern copy of an ancient painting in the tomb of an official named Rekhmire at Thebes from 1504–1425 BCE. Painted on paper at Thebes by artist Nina de Garis Davies in 1932 for the Met, obj. no. 33.8.3.

**Gold sandals** from 1479–1425 BCE. Made of hammered sheets of gold. Probably from the tomb of three wives of the king Tuthmosis III in Thebes. Purchased by the Met, obj. no. 26.8.146.

## The Launderer

Background image: **The Nile River at Luxor**. Photo by Marc Ryckaert.

**Bucket** from the 4th–7th centuries CE. Made of pottery. Purchased by the Met, obj. no. 25.10.23.98.

**Painting of people doing their laundry on the banks of the Nile** from the late 19th or early 20th century by Emil Uhl. Made with oil paint on canvas. Photo by Wikipedia user WolfD59.

**Photograph of people doing their laundry on the banks of the Nile** from a late 19th or early 20th century postcard. From the collection of Dr. Paula Sanders. Photo by Wikipedia user BumpySlug.

## The Bird Catcher

Background image: **Egyptian geese**. Photo by Fanny Schertzer, uploaded by Wikipedia user Inisheer.

**Statue of a woman holding a duck and carrying a basket of meat on her head** from 1981–1975 BCE. Made of painted wood and plaster. Excavated at Thebes in the tomb of an official named Meketre by a team of archaeologists from the Met, obj. no. 20.3.7.

**Man hunting birds with a clapnet**. Modern copy of an ancient painting in the tomb of an official named Khnumhotep at Beni Hasan from 1897–1878 BCE. Painted on paper at Beni Hasan by artist Nina de Garis Davies in 1931 for the Met, obj. no. 33.8.18.

**Man carrying ducks** from 1550–1295 BCE. Made of painted plaster. Donated to the Met, obj. no. 06.1332.1.

**Throw stick** from 1981–1802 BCE. Made of wood. Excavated in a tomb at Meir and later purchased by the Met, obj. no. 12.182.67.

**The official Menna and his family hunting in the marshes**. Modern copy of an ancient painting in the tomb of an official named Menna at Thebes from 1400–

1352 BCE. Painted on paper at Thebes by artist Nina de Garis Davies in 1924 for the Met, obj. no. 30.4.48.

# The Fisherman

Background image: **The Nile River at sunset**. Photo © Vyacheslav Argenberg / www.vascoplanet.com.

**Men preparing fish**. Modern copy of an ancient painting in the tomb of an official named Puimre at Thebes from 1479–1458 BCE. Painted on paper at Thebes by artist Hugh R. Hopgood in 1914–1916 for the Met, obj. no. 30.4.17.

**Ostracon showing the god Sobek** from 1295–1070 BCE. Made of limestone with writing in ink. Purchased by the Met, obj. no. 29.2.23.

**Crocodile amulet** from 304–247 BCE. Made of faience (a type of ceramic). Donated to the Met, obj. no. 1989.281.96.

**Makeup palette in the shape of a fish** from 3650–3300 BCE. Made of greywacke (a type of stone). Purchased by the Met, obj. no. 07.228.61.

# Wisdom

Photo: **Birth chapel of Hatshepsut at Philae Temple** by Jorge Láscar.

# Be a Scribe!

Background image: **Pyramids at Abusir**. Photo © Vyacheslav Argenberg / www.vascoplanet.com.

**Statue of the royal scribe Horemhab (future king)** from 1336–1323 BCE. Made of granodiorite (a type of stone). Donated to the Met, obj. no. 23.10.1.

**Necklace** from 1390–1352 BCE. Made of faience (a type of ceramic), bronze, glass, and stones called agate, carnelian, lapis lazuli, and turquoise. Excavated in a house at Thebes by the Met, obj. no. 11.215.450.

**The Temple of Hathor at Serabit el-Khadim in the Sinai desert**. Photo by Wikipedia user Einsamer Schütze.

**Scribe's pen case** from 1045–992 BCE. Made of wood, reed, and ink. Purchased by the Met, obj. no. 47.123.

**Stone with early alphabetic writing from Serabit el-Khadim in the Sinai desert**. Photo by Wikipedia user Oxfordus167 (photo background removed).

# Stay Out of Trouble

Background image: **Mudbrick wall at Luxor**. Photo by Marc Ryckaert.

**Elephant ivory tusk**. Located at the Warther Museum in Dover, Ohio. Photo by Flickr user James St. John (photo background removed).

**Jar label with the name of the king Den** from 2960–2770 BCE. Made of inscribed ebony wood. Excavated in the tomb of the king Den at Abydos and then donated to the BM, obj. no. EA32650.

**Siwa Oasis**. Photo by Wikipedia user Vincent Battesti.

**Brick** from 1279–1213 BCE. Made of faience (a type of ceramic). Purchased by the Met, obj. no. 66.99.114.

**Modern Egyptian chewing gum** (the label says "Chiclets" in Arabic). Photo by Bethany Simpson.

**Gum arabic**. Photo by Wikipedia user Gixie (photo background removed).

**Gum arabic leaking from a babhul tree**. Photo by Wikipedia user Ashwin Baindur (photo cropped).

# Mind Your Manners

Background image: **Nile River**. Photo by Ron Porter.

**Chair belonging to a scribe named Reniseneb** from about 1450 BCE. Made of wood, ebony wood, and ivory. Purchased by the Met, obj. no. 68.58.

**Djehutyemhab and his wife Baketkhonsu receiving funerary offerings in the afterlife**. Modern copy of an ancient painting in the tomb of an official named Djehutyemhab at Thebes from 1279–1213 BCE. Painted on paper at Thebes by artist Norman de Garis Davies in 1908 for the Met, obj. no. 15.5.15.

**Low table** from 2750–2649 BCE. Made of travertine (a type of stone, also called Egyptian alabaster). Excavated in a tomb at Saqqara and then purchased by the Met, obj. no. 12.181.174.

**Table** from 1539–1292 BCE. Made of wood. Purchased by the Brooklyn Museum in New York (www.brooklynmuseum.org) using the Charles Edwin Wilbour Fund, obj. no. 37.41E. Photo © Brooklyn Museum.

# Don't Blab!

Background image: **Palm grove**. Photo by diego_cue.

**Sculpture of the head of an official** from 1390–1352 BCE. Made of granodiorite (a type of stone). Purchased by the Met, obj. no. 66.99.27.

**Ceremonial shield belonging to the king Tutankhamun** from 1336–1327 BCE. Made of painted wood and gold. Excavated at Thebes in the tomb of Tutankhamun and later brought to the Grand Egyptian Museum (www.grandegyptianmuseum.org), obj. no. JE1576.

**The scribe Nakht overseeing people working on his estate**. Modern copy of an ancient painting in the tomb of Nakht at Thebes from 1410–1370 BCE. Painted on paper at Thebes by the artists Norman de Garis Davies and Lancelot Crane from 1907–1910 for the Met, obj. no. 15.5.19.

**Statue of a guardian** from 1919–1885 BCE. Made of painted wood and plaster. Excavated in the tomb of an official named Imhotep at Lisht by a team of archaeologists from the Met, obj. no. 14.3.17.

**Statue of an official named Mitry** from 2381–2323 BCE. Made of painted wood and plaster. Excavated at Saqqara in the tomb of Mitry and later purchased by the Met, obj. no. 26.2.4.

# Don't Play Hooky

Background image: **Buildings at el-Qasr**. Photo © NYU Excavations at Amheida / Institute for the Study of the Ancient World.

**Scribes from a model of a granary** from 1981–1975 BCE. Made of painted wood, plaster, and linen fabric. Excavated at Thebes in the tomb of an official named Meketre by a team of archaeologists from the Met, obj. no. 20.3.11.

**Four scribes at work** from 1350–1333 BCE. Made of painted limestone. From the National Archaeological Museum in Florence, Italy, obj. no. 2566.

**Writing board** from 1981–1802 BCE. Made of painted wood, plaster, and ink. Purchased by the Met, obj. no. 28.9.4.

# Follow Orders

Background image: **River rushes in Luxor**. Photo by Wikipedia user jrtaylor08.

**Jar for liquid** from 1492–1473 BCE. Made of travertine (a type of stone, also called Egyptian alabaster). Excavated at Thebes in the tomb of Hatnefer and Ramose by a team of archaeologists from the Met, obj. no. 36.3.1.

**The official Rekhmire and his mother receiving offerings in the afterlife**. Modern copy of an ancient painting in the tomb of an official named Rekhmire at Thebes from 1504–1425 BCE. Painted on paper at Thebes by artist Charles K. Wilkinson in 1928–1929 for the Met, obj. no. 30.4.79.

**Cylinder seal** from 2960–2770 BCE. Made of ivory. Purchased by the Met, obj. no. 10.130.1600.

**Scarab inscribed with a person's name** from 1550–1458 BCE. Made of red jasper or carnelian (two types of stone). Excavated at Thebes and later purchased by the Met, obj. no. 26.7.308.

**Jar with handles** from 1070–1000 BCE. Made of pottery. Excavated at Thebes in the tomb of the queen Ahmose-Meritamun by a team of archaeologists from the Met, obj. no. 30.3.42.

**Signet ring with Tutankhamun's name** from 1336–1327 BCE. Made of gold. Purchased by the Met, obj. no. 22.9.3.

## Control Yourself

Background image: **The Nile River at Aswan**.

**Head of a goddess, probably Mut** from around 700 BCE. Made of a copper alloy, this figurehead was probably designed to be attached to the prow of a processional barque—a small ship used in festivals for the gods. Purchased by the Met, obj. no. 2008.353.

**Balance scale** from 500–600 CE. Made of bronze. Purchased by the Met, obj. no. 14.2.2.

**Men making tiger nut cakes.** Modern copies of ancient paintings in the tomb of an official named Rekhmire at Thebes from 1504–1425 BCE. Painted on paper at Thebes by artist Nina de Garis Davies in 1927 for the Met, obj. nos. 31.6.16, 31.6.17, 31.6.24, 31.6.30, and 31.6.31.

## Be Gumptious

Background image: **The Edge of the Cultivation in Upper Egypt**.

**A seated official** from 2010–1981 BCE. Made of painted limestone. Excavated at Thebes in the tomb of an official named Dagi by the Met, obj. no. 12.180.243.

**Ipuy and his wife Duammeres receiving funerary offerings from their children.** Modern copy of an ancient painting in the tomb of a sculptor named Ipuy at Thebes from 1295–1213 BCE. Painted on paper at Thebes by artist Norman de Garis Davies in 1920–1921 for the Met, obj. no. 30.4.114.

**Letter written in cuneiform** from 1353–1336 BCE. Made of pottery. Purchased by the Met, obj. no. 24.2.12.

**Letter written in hieratic** from 1479–1458 BCE. Made of papyrus with writing in ink. Excavated in the temple of Hatshepsut at Deir el-Bahari in Thebes by a team of archaeologists from the Met, obj. no. 27.3.560.

## Fate Is Your Friend

Background image: **Mortuary Temple of Hatshepsut at Deir el-Bahari**. Photo by Diego Delso, delso.photo, License CC-BY-SA.

**The goddess Meskhenet** from 332–30 BCE. Carved into a wall at Kom Obmo temple. Photo by Carole Reeves.

**Scene from a Book of the Dead belonging to a singer and priestess named Nauny** from about 1050 BCE. Made of painted papyrus. Excavated at Thebes in the tomb of the queen Ahmose-Meritamun by a team of archaeologists from the Met, obj. no. 30.3.31.

**Stela with the goddess Meskhenet as a brick with a woman's face** from 1292–1190 BCE. Made of painted limestone. Located at the Egyptian Museum in Turin (https://collezioni.museoegizio.it/en-GB), obj. no. 1658.

## Endpapers

Pattern from Owen Jones. *The Grammar of Ornament. Illustrated by Examples from various Styles of Ornament. One Hundred folio Plates. Drawn on Stone* by F. Bedford. London: Day and Son, 1856.

# About the Authors

### Michael Hoffen

Michael Hoffen is the youngest-ever recipient of the annual Emerson Prize, awarded by the *Concord Review* for outstanding promise in history. While still in middle school, he was introduced to the joys of translating ancient texts and never looked back. During the pandemic, Michael decided to embark on an ambitious project to bring ancient Egyptian literature to life outside the classroom. *Be a Scribe!* is Michael's first book in a series intended for young readers. He is extraordinarily grateful for the opportunity to work with Callaway Publications. When not chasing down new stories to translate or write, Michael enjoys hiking, swimming, and rock climbing.

### Christian Casey

Dr. Christian Casey is an Egyptologist who specializes in the study of ancient Egyptian languages. He obtained his PhD in Egyptology from Brown University in 2020 and now works as a researcher at Freie Universität Berlin. He is especially interested in sharing the exciting world of ancient Egypt with young people and other interested members of the public.

### Jen Thum

Dr. Jen Thum is an Egyptologist, educator, and curator at the Harvard Art Museums. She received her degrees in Egyptology and Archaeology from the University of Oxford and Brown University. Jen's work and research center on how people learn from art and artifacts. She teaches at the Harvard Graduate School of Education, publishes widely about learning with ancient objects, and is the lead editor of *Teaching Ancient Egypt in Museums: Pedagogies in Practice*. Jen conceived of *Be a Scribe!* after recognizing the need for accessible ancient Egyptian primary sources for young learners.

## Follow Us

**Michael Hoffen**
TikTok: @michaelthescribe or https://www.tiktok.com/@michaelthescribe
Instagram: @michaelthescribe or https://www.instagram.com/michaelthescribe
Facebook: Michael Hoffen or https://www.facebook.com/michaelhoffenscribe

**Christian Casey**
Instagram: @Osarnachthis or https://www.instagram.com/osarnachthis

**Jen Thum**
Instagram: @egyptolojen or https://www.instagram.com/egyptolojen

# INDEX

**A**

*Aamu* 14, 50, 51
Abydos 12, 15
adobe 39, 67
adzes 28, 29
amulets 21, 35, 61
Amun 30
Anubis 81
*Areryt* 80, 81
arrows 48, 53
artistic skill 26, 30, 31

**B**

barber 32, 33
beatings 20, 44, 46, 72
beer 75, 76
bees 32, 33, 43
bird catcher 58, 59
birds 34, 58, 59, 60
boats 18, 19, 21, 34, 35
Book of the Dead 12, 81
bows 31, 48
bread 37, 38, 46, 47, 76, 77
brick 38, 39, 50, 51, 66, 67, 80, 81
bronze 27, 32, 49

**C**

Canaan 14, 65
Canaanites 65
capital 6, 18, 19, 20, 64, 65, 67, 71, 74
carnelian 31
carpenter 28, 29
ceramic. *See* pottery
chariots 53
chisels 30
clapnet 58
clothes 22, 36, 46, 52, 56
copper 27, 28, 31
coriander 42, 43
corvée labor 44, 45
courier 50, 51
crocodiles 26, 27, 56, 57, 60, 61, 80
crucibles 26, 27
cubit 40, 41
cuneiform 79

**D**

Delta 14, 18, 34, 35, 44, 45, 65

**E**

ebony 66, 67

**F**

Faiyum Oasis 14
farmer 28, 44, 45, 64, 69
fate 66, 80
fathers 6, 20, 23, 80
fish 26, 27, 58, 59, 60, 61
fisherman 60, 61
forges 26, 27

**G**

gardener 42, 43
gods and goddesses 30, 31, 60, 61, 64, 76, 80, 81
gold 15, 26, 27, 30, 31, 54, 55
grain 22, 23, 44, 47
grapes 42, 43
gum 67

**H**

harpoons 60
heart 20, 21, 50, 75, 76, 81
Hierakonpolis 15
*hin* 74, 75, 76
houses 36, 39, 40, 41, 48, 50, 68, 69

**I**

inlay 30
Itjtawy 14, 19
ivory 66, 67, 74

**J**

javelins 49
jeweler 30, 31

**K**

Karnak 15
*Kemyt* 20, 21
Khety 6, 18, 20, 21, 29, 33, 43, 45, 51, 52, 55, 57, 59, 61, 64, 65, 66, 67, 71, 75, 80
kilts 22, 23, 53, 71

**L**

lamps 28, 29
lapis lazuli 30, 31

95

launderer 56, 57
leather 52, 53, 54, 55
leather worker 52, 53
Lebanon 14, 29, 79
letters 21, 51, 65, 74, 78, 79, 81
lions 44, 50, 55
loincloths 22, 38
lord 44, 51, 68, 69
Lower Egypt 14

## M

map 18, 19, 34, 35
Meskhenet 80, 81
metal 26, 27, 31
mines 14, 31, 64, 65
mirror 32
models 18, 19, 22, 36, 37, 39, 40, 43, 44, 46, 48, 72, 73
molds 26, 27, 37, 38, 39
month 40, 41
mosquitoes 34, 35
mothers 22, 75, 76, 80
mudbrick. *See* brick
Mut 76

## N

names 31, 59, 74, 75
nets 58, 60
Nile 14, 15, 18, 19, 34, 35, 49, 56, 57, 60, 61, 65
Nubia 15

## O

oases 14, 15, 67
officials 18, 19, 39, 68, 69, 70, 71, 74, 76, 78
oil 29
ore 30, 31
Osiris 81
ostracon (plural: ostraca) 12, 21
outskirts 48, 49, 50

## P

papyrus 9, 11, 12, 23, 34, 59, 73, 80, 81
Pepi 6, 18, 71
pigs 36
potter 36, 37, 38
pottery 21, 27, 29, 36, 37, 61

## Q

quivers 48, 53

## R

ravens 44
razors 32, 33
Re 30, 31

Red Sea 15
river. *See* Nile
roofer 40, 41

## S

sandal maker 54, 55
sandals 54, 55
sandstorms 38
scale 76
scarabs
  heart 21, 75
scepters 71
school 23, 72, 73
scribe 18, 20, 22, 23, 27, 29, 60, 61, 64, 65, 72, 73, 74, 78
sculptor 26
shields 48, 70
shoulder-yokes 42, 43
Sile 14, 18, 65
Sinai 14, 64, 65
smith 26, 27
Sobek 61, 80
spears 48, 59

## T

tables 68, 69
taxes 20, 44, 45, 68
tenant farmer 44, 45, 69
tents 51
Thebes 15, 19
throwsticks 59
tomb scenes 20, 26, 28, 30, 31, 32, 33, 34, 35, 37, 38, 39, 42, 43, 44, 45, 47, 48, 50, 51, 53, 54, 55, 58, 59, 61, 69, 71, 73, 74, 75, 77, 79
trader 34, 35
turquoise 14, 31, 64
Tutankhamun 70, 75
tweezers 32
Tyre 79

## U

Upper Egypt 15, 19, 34

## V

Valley of the Kings 15
viziers 68

## W

wall builder 38, 39, 40, 41
weapon maker 48, 49
weaver 46, 47
whetstones 32
wisdom texts 18, 21, 73
women 33, 46, 47, 52, 53, 80
wood 14, 18, 22, 28, 29, 40, 41, 43, 44, 46, 48, 49, 66, 69, 72, 73

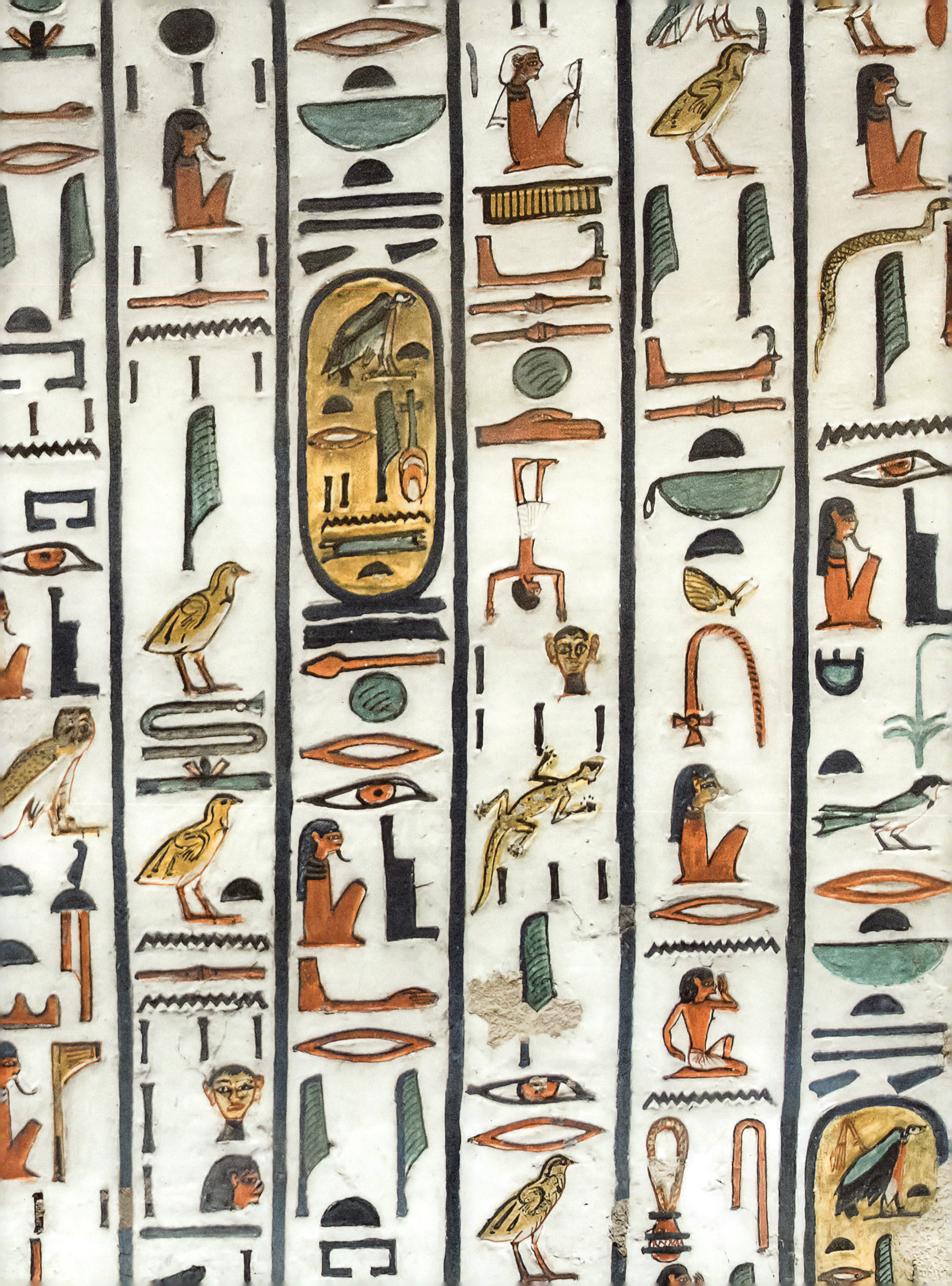